For
Katherine, Drew, Will, and Lucy
Third Generation Disney Fans

Contents

Introduction

Disneyland will never be completed. It will continue to grow as long as there is imagination left in the world.

—Walt Disney

As far as Walt was concerned, Disneyland was "the star" of his entertainment empire. "Everything else," he said, "is in the supporting role." The park was an incredibly special personal achievement, the place where his hopes, dreams, and ambitions came to life right alongside costumed character versions of his classic cartoons. Something the park wasn't known for, not until the opening of New Orleans Square in 1966, was superlative foods and beverages.

You may have heard the origin stories, how as a young father with two active daughters, he wanted to share with them a weekend outing suitable for the whole family to enjoy together. He knew what he *didn't* want—no ill-kept, lackluster, under-maintained carnival-style rides and games of chance staffed by unsavory employees who went about their work as if it were the *last* thing on earth they wanted to be doing. He became disenchanted taking his girls to places where Diane and Sharon went on the rides while Dad sat on a bench and watched and waved at them. Disneyland was his answer to the dilemma.

With his film and television enterprises off and running, he first cast his eye on an undeveloped little corner of land near his studio in Burbank, California. It wasn't much, but he thought with some imagination and elbow grease, he could turn it into a pleasant place for families to share a Sunday afternoon where his beloved animated characters could come to life and interact with the public and where rides would be designed to appeal to guests of all ages.

Eventually, with the expert help of consultants, he decided that particular parcel was too small to accommodate his big dream. The little undeveloped corner is now home to the Walt Disney Animation Studios and ABC. He needed at least 160 acres for a theme park, enough room for the place to grow over the years. After World War II, Southern California was booming. I know because I grew up there myself, right along with Disneyland. Every bit of land was quickly being snapped up by developers. Orange groves soon gave way to housing tracts and schools, just like the one down the street from my house that became Ceres Elementary School.

Ultimately, Anaheim some thirty-seven miles east of his Burbank studio was the site he selected. Other areas, for one reason or another, didn't make the final cut. There were too many local restrictions and regulations, the land owners wanted too much money for their property, access wasn't supported by the freeway system. Once he had the land, he needed to raise the funds, and that proved an even more ponderous task than selecting a locale. Banks weren't at all convinced that something entirely new like a theme park was any sort of a sure thing. Still, this was something he believed in so strongly that he was willing to borrow against his personal life insurance policy and sell his Smoke Tree Ranch home in Palm Springs. Finally, ABC agreed to invest if Walt Disney would create a television program for the incipient network, and he did. Not surprisingly, he called the show Disneyland.

Construction started on July 16, 1954, and on July 17, 1955, the main gates opened. The initial cost was the oft-quoted figure of $17 million. By today's standards, that financial outlay seems relatively modest. Keep in mind that the venture's success was far from assured, although it is difficult to imagine today how fiscally precarious those early years truly were. Nothing like Disneyland had been done, let alone done well. Still, by 1960, Disney owned all the shares in Disneyland. By August 1, 1995, the New York Times reported:

> In the second-largest corporate takeover ever, the Walt Disney
> Company moved yesterday to create the world's most power-
> ful media and entertainment company, announcing that it
> would acquire Capital Cities/ ABC Inc. for $19 billion.

From then on, and with a number of cyclical ups and downs,
the global entertainment juggernaut known as Disney and the
Disneyland theme parks have continued to move forward just
as Walt Disney dreamed they would so many decades ago. "As
long as there is imagination left in the world," as he aptly put
it, they always will.

I was there as a four-year-old the summer Disneyland
opened, not on opening day when you either had to have
a special invitation or be a member of the press, but shortly
thereafter and every season following that summer during
the years I spent growing up in Southern California, going to
college, and starting a family. The early years were every bit
as exciting as you'd imagine, and nothing felt quite as special
as the opening of a new attraction like the Matterhorn which
we watched as it rose to tower over the Santa Ana Freeway,
usually referred to as the 5, or the creation of an entirely new
land like New Orleans Square. We went often and enthusias-
tically took out-of-town visitors on tours, proudly showing off
what felt like our own personal park.

Working there was always a dream for me, and when my
cousin got a position as a sweeper at a time when that job was
exclusively for men, it whetted my appetite. He came home
with thrilling descriptions of what went on "backstage" and
anecdotes about insiders-only fun like cast member canoe
races, cast baseball games, and the Parking Lot Olympics. Very
late one evening after the gates had closed and the guests had
gone home, he even ran into Walt Disney himself strolling the
deserted streets keeping a careful eye on things. They greeted
each other with a nod using first names, something Walt
insisted on from sweepers right on up to the man in charge.
It seemed impossibly glamorous, and I couldn't wait to start
working there myself!

If you'd like to hear more about the early years from a cast
member's perspective, I've written about my college years from
1969 through 1972 in *The Cream of the Crop: Tour Guide Tales*

from Disneyland's Golden Years, published by Theme Park Press. I handed out carnations at the Main Gate for Disneyland's big 15th anniversary, carefully steered my tour groups around throngs of Hippies and Yippies who took over the park on August 6, 1970, and took a very young David Geffen, Jackson Browne, and Joni Mitchell on a memorable VIP tour in 1972 around the time he made a major deal merging his Asylum Records label with Elektra.

Disneyland was known for many things back in the early days, but good food was very definitely not one of them! Burgers and fries, Coke, ice cream bars, popcorn—yes. Typical "fair" food, what we now call fast food, was widely available. Something more inventive or substantial than that—not so much. When the Blue Bayou opened with New Orleans Square on July 24, 1966, it was a real revelation. The menu was extensive and inventive, especially when compared with what had gone before, and it actually tasted *good*. Better than good, in some cases.

The first time my cousin took us all for lunch at the Bayou, we marveled at the golden, crispy, heavenly-tasting Monte Cristo sandwich cut carefully into four wedges (these days, only three) served in a cloth napkin, dusted lightly with powdered sugar, and accompanied by fresh fruit and berry jam. As we sat in perpetual blue twilight by the river listening to the screams of guests in the boats heading over the falls to the brand-new Pirates of the Caribbean attraction, it was clear that Disneyland had made a definite sea change as far as cuisine was concerned. Dining would never be the same again in our favorite theme park. Since that day, eating at drinking at Disneyland has followed a sharply upward trajectory.

Today, you'll be treated to a wealth of exceptional dining opportunities. Meeting and greeting the characters is always a thrill, but sometimes the lines are prohibitively tedious. Have a bountiful brunch in the Magic Kingdom with costumed characters like Minnie Mouse and her friends at the Plaza Inn, try the new Disney Princess Breakfast Adventures at Napa Rose, or sit down for dinner with Goofy and his pals at the Disneyland Hotel. Every character comes to every table to chat, pose for photos, and sign autographs with no waiting in queues whatsoever.

For upscale dining on a level Walt could hardly have imagined back in the 1950s, think about booking a chef's table for dinner at the Napa Rose in Disney's Grand Californian Hotel with Chef Andrew Sutton where you'll feast on the finest, freshest foods California has to offer, accompanied by a wine list carefully chosen to complement each dish to perfection. Chef also serves up beautiful haute cuisine at Carthay Circle inside Disney California Adventure if you find yourself craving a very special lunch or dinner during your visit.

A casual day out with the family or friends, but you'd still like something seriously yummy? Not to worry, Fantasyland's Red Rose Tavern has exquisite choices. The Beast's Forbidden Burger, Chef's Chopped Salad with Grilled Chicken, or Chicken Sandwich à la Lumière are all dandy, especially when followed by the decadent Grey Stuff Gâteau. The corn dogs at DCA's Corn Dog Castle are spectacular. New Orleans Square restaurants have many authentic Creole specialties to tempt you, and you can get an espresso from the same machine that served Walt Disney to go with your Mickey-shaped beignets at the Café Orleans. Dine on out-of-this world specialties in Star Wars: Galaxy's Edge like Roasted Endorian Tip-Yip Salad, Smoked Kaadu Ribs, or a plant-based Felucian Garden Spread.

Don't forget the many offerings waiting for you *between* the two theme parks, either. At Downtown Disney, you'll discover goodies you just won't find inside the Main Gates. Mexican specialties at Catal or Tortilla Jo's are spicy enough to be interesting but still friendly to most palates. Ralph Brennan's Jazz Kitchen is lively, fun, and filled with Southern specialties. Look for house-made brews at Ballast Point Brewing Co., check out the wild new ice cream varieties at Salt and Straw, and Sprinkles always has you covered with world-famous cupcakes galore.

Dining at Disneyland was never like this back when the park was young, but today there's a whole new world of flavors and treats just waiting to tempt you. Turn the page and dig in!

CHAPTER ONE

About the Dining Reviews

In the following chapters, the cost of eating at each Disney quick-service or table-service restaurant is indicated with a range of prices:

$ = $14.99 and lower
$$ = $15-$34.99
$$$= $35-$59.99
$$$$ = $60 and higher

Depending on how finicky you are, you can enjoy a good meal at the low end of the range or splurge on the high. Of course, Disney frequently changes its prices—usually upwards—so if cost is a crucial factor in your decision to eat at a specific restaurant, check the menu beforehand. For up-to-the-minute, guaranteed accurate information, you should check only the menus on the official Disneyland website: disneyland.disney.go.com Only use the menus cribbed on Disney fan sites or on unauthorized, unofficial apps with caution.

As of now, Disneyland no longer offers pre-paid Disneyland Dining Plans or Meal Vouchers. Before your stay, telephone the Disneyland Resort at (714) 781-4636 for the best, most up-to-date information on this topic. If you want to make a dining reservation, telephone (714) 781-3463; that's (714)-781-DINE. You may do so up to 60 days before you want to book. It's also possible to book online right on the official Disneyland website: disneyland.disney.go.com. You'll enter the number of guests in your party, the meal of your choice (breakfast, brunch, lunch, or dinner), and a time you'd like to dine. If there's an opening, you'll know right away or be given possible alternative choices as close as possible to the time requested.

As with any restaurant, prices at Disneyland eateries and menu items change without warning. Lots of the food choices are seasonal, so there are always novel specialties to reflect the freshest ingredients in every season of the year. Chefs like to keep things unique and exciting, so at the very best Disney dining venues, you'll see even more frequent rollouts of new creations to tempt the palate. You can always count on many of your favorite, familiar kinds of Disney goodies, but any guidebook like this one is meant to give you an idea of the kind of foods you may find on your visit, not any specific menu because those will change quite frequently. Once you've booked your hotel reservation or when you know you'll be in the area, that's the time to check the official website for a menu. Even then, however, you may well discover an entirely new menu in place once you arrive. The only way to be absolutely certain of what's being served at a particular dining place is to consult the official website on the day of your reservation.

Unless otherwise indicated, the cost range given for each restaurant is per adult. If the restaurant offers an Annual Passport Discount, you'll see the designation "APD" after the cost range. Most people who buy them live in the area or visit Anaheim so frequently that it makes sense to spring for one.

A word to the wise about the latest trend: Mobile Orders. Download the Disneyland Dining App on your mobile device. You can pre-select and pre-order your food and beverage choices at some places so that when you arrive at the restaurant, everything is ready (or close to ready) for you at a special pick-up area. This is a great time-saver, and with a little practice you'll gain confidence and become adept at doing this. Be sure to check at the time of your visit, because more and more places are adding this option—and it's a good one!

Reservations are always recommended at table-service restaurants. At the more popular places, like Napa Rose, The Blue Bayou, and Goofy's Kitchen, reservations might as well be required, as they're snapped up so quickly. Any character meal with the Disney gang is highly desirable and, as a result, that much harder to book. Since Napa Rose located in the Grand Californian Hotel rolled out the new Disney Princess

Breakfast Adventures in March of 2019, that's become one of the most coveted reservations at the resort.

During less busy seasons, you might get lucky as a walk-up and score a table. It never hurts to try. But if you know your dining plans in advance, avoid possible disappointment and book yourself a reservation. Priority when making a reservation is given to guests staying at one of the three Disneyland Resort Hotels: The Grand Californian, The Disneyland Hotel, or The Paradise Pier Hotel.

It's like reading a manufacturer's warranty, isn't it? I don't know about you, but I've already built up an appetite...

CHAPTER TWO

Main Street, U.S.A.

As Walt Disney first envisioned the grand entrance to his theme park, it was to be a typical, apple-pie slice of Americana at the turn of the century, the *twentieth* century, that is. It was a snapshot of a simpler world, a slower time before everything in our lives became so very complicated and rushed. It was a bit of Marceline, Missouri, where Walt and his brother, Roy, spent some of their happiest growing-up years. It was also a bit of the Henry Ford Museum with its Greenfield Village, a place he had visited a couple of times not long before conceiving of what Disneyland would look like. Throw in some Ft. Collins Colorado, a place where legendary Disneyland designer Harper Goff was raised, and you'll have a good idea of how Main Street, U.S.A. came to be. Look for Main Street, too, as you watch the animated classic *Lady and the Tramp*, a film released less than a month before the park opened. Much of it will look familiar.

It funnels guests into the other lands with the pink and blue Sleeping Beauty castle beckoning them forward at its end. With a forced perspective, the castle is actually smaller than it appears. No matter. It's the iconic symbol of Disney, one that has stood the test of time. Take an old-time, horse-drawn trolley, one of the original seventeen attractions on opening day, July 17, 1955. Time was, before lettered tickets for the attractions became ephemera and faded into history, a ride on the trolley cost an A ticket, one thin dime. The slow clop-clop of the big draft horse's hooves echoed hollowly on the asphalt, just as they did back in the "olden days." Two of them ran simultaneously, one up and one down the street. Now, usually one trolley runs and, in busy times, trolleys don't run at all. Look for the place where the rails divide about halfway up the street and you'll see where the plodding horses used to pass side by side. If you do see a horse working, don't feel sorry for it. Disneyland horses are among the most well cared-for equines on the planet. They work no more than four hours per day, four days per week. Honey-gold Clydesdales, gleaming black Belgians, and dappled gray Percherons wear comfortable, rubber-soled shoes. It would be difficult to find horses anywhere more loved and pampered.

Old-time fire engines, an omnibus, vintage automobiles, high-stepping bobbed-tailed Hackney ponies pulling carts, and other conveyances typical of the 1900s used to be frequently seen up and down the street. These days, those are rarely, and some of them never, brought out of mothballs. At one time, the Circle D coral on the property housed herds of many more horses and mules from the Mule Train ride than it does now. Just as in the history books, they've been put out to pasture; that land was recently used in the creation of Star Wars: Galaxy's Edge.

The town square boasts two cannons, possibly a gift from the local D.A.R., as the song goes in *The Music Man*? Uh, no, these are French army cannons never fired in battle. A tall flagpole is the site of flag-raising and flag-lowering ceremonies daily. The old gas lamps were originally from Baltimore. Up and down the street are second-story windows dedicated to Disney Legends. Walt's personal apartment, decorated in lavish red and gold Victorian style by Lillian Disney, is located over the fire station. Look for a light always burning at night in the window in memory of the great man himself.

After more than sixty years, the old street has recently undergone some significant changes for the first time in its history. Regardless, what *won't* change it the message on the little bronze plaque that still lets visitors know Walt's original intent: ~DISNEYLAND~ To all who come to this happy place WELCOME. Disneyland is your land. Here age relives fond memories of the past...And here youth may savor the challenges and promise of the future. Disneyland is dedicated to the dreams, the ideals, and the hard facts that have created America...with the hope that it will be a source of joy and inspiration to all the World. July 17, 1955.

Main Street, U.S.A., Kiosks, Wagons, and Carts

Note: You can count on finding bottles of water just about anywhere food is sold, so I won't mention that fact every time I discuss menus. Because of renovations that may be going on, some of the mobile food purveyors may be located in slightly different places. What you can always count on, however, is the fact that there will be plenty of food available on Main Street!

- Two **Churro Carts** are generally in operation daily, one at the top of the central hub and one on Town Square. While the Magic Kingdom at Walt Disney World in Florida only has two carts in all, Disneyland has at least eight with another four and sometimes five more at Disney California Adventure and Downtown Disney. The 16-inch-long churros are fresh and warm and come in lots of flavors. They've become a cult classic.

- Just past the central hub to the left, you'll find a little **Coffee** stand that should do nicely if you haven't had time for breakfast. Chocolate croissants, butter croissants, cinnamon twists, muffins (Double chocolate chip! Blueberry sour cream!), and all kinds of coffee, cocoa, and other beverages are available.

- The **Little Red Wagon** near the Plaza Inn on your right as you head towards the castle sells premium, all-beef, hand-dipped corn dogs that will knock your socks off, along with chips or apple slices and Coke products.

- Walk past the Market House and you'll come to a little side street. Here, there's a lovely **Fresh Fruit** stand loaded with healthy snacks like whole fruit, a berry bowl, sliced apples with caramel dip, veggies with dip, hummus, watermelon slices, seedless grapes, pineapple spears, dill pickles, and more. There are also beverages including orange juice.

- Find two **Ice Cream Carts** on Main Street. The one by the Plaza Inn has Nestle Dibs (bite-sized shareable little pieces of Nestle's crunch-chocolate-coated vanilla ice cream), Häagen-Daz ice cream bars, frozen lemonade (try this if you haven't already!), and cotton candy, while the one on the other side of the street just past the entrance to Adventureland sells the classic Premium Mickey ice cream bars, a chocolate chip cookie ice cream sandwich, frozen bananas (a park must-try!), a strawberry fruit bar, and other ice cream and frozen lemonade novelties.

- There are two **Popcorn Carts** on the street, one near Town Square as you enter the park and the other on the central hub. Popcorn has been a part of Disneyland since the beginning, but it's no longer ten cents a box. Large, refillable, collectible containers have soared in popularity—and price—as of late.

- **Jumbo Turkey Legs** are another park favorite. There's a stand on the central hub where you can pick up this filling snack, along with corn on the cob (buttered or with lime/chili), a chimichanga, large bag of chips, and Coke products.

Carnation Café

APD: Yes, Cost: $-$$
TYPE: American, Table Service; Breakfast, Lunch, Dinner

Located about halfway down Main Street on your left facing the castle, look for the red and white striped umbrellas that signal your arrival at the Carnation Café. As with several of the Main Street dining establishments, there are indoor or outdoor seating areas. Make reservations as soon as you know you're coming. They're highly recommended!

Breakfast is standard American fare like ham and eggs, pancakes, and steel-cut oatmeal, but there are some appealing less usual menu items, too, like eggs Benedict, a spinach and tomato egg-white frittata, country fried steak and eggs, and Mickey waffles with strawberry or apple topping sided with sausage links or bacon. For lighter appetites, try the vanilla yogurt, granola, parfait with fruit. Just now, and for a limited time, there's a "Celebrate Mickey" chicken and waffle. Disney Check meals for kids include a seasonal fruit plate or the all-American breakfast.

Lunch and dinner menus and prices are similar—T.V. Dinner Pot Roast is only for dinner. Fried dill pickles coated in Parmesan and panko with dipping sauce are a great starter, and so is the popular baked potato soup loaded with cheddar cheese, bacon, sour cream, and chives. It's delicious and so filling you might just skip the entrée. Walt's chili (and he actually was a big chili fan) is a hearty choice. Seasonal shrimp salad and a grilled chicken and fresh spinach salad are healthful meal choices. Sandwiches include roast turkey, an Angus beef cheeseburger (Oregon Tillamook—yum!) on a brioche roll that's pretty irresistible, or a veggie burger, and each comes with either fries or fresh fruit. Try penne pasta with shrimp, fried chicken, fish, and meatloaf, all of which are filling and satisfying, but if you can manage to save room for dessert, you won't regret it!

This old-fashioned American-style café has some malts, ice cream sundaes, milk shakes, ice cream floats, and seasonal cheesecakes. Kids have two Disney check choices, a seasonal fruit plate and a PB & J build-your-own sandwich plus the more traditional mac and cheese, fried chicken, and a hamburger. This café is a good option for families looking to fill up the troops without breaking the bank. The food is good and nicely prepared, the choices are extensive enough to please most, and the mood is casual.

Gibson Girl Ice Cream Parlor

ADP: No, Cost: $
TYPE: American, Quick Service, Mobile Orders; Snacks

Travel back to a time about a hundred and twenty years ago when dapper young guys in bow ties and straw boater hats treated their best girls to a strawberry sundae at the local soda shop. You'll find lots of old-fashioned frozen goodies here from hand-scooped cones (plain, waffle, or chocolate dipped) or cups with plenty of sprinkles and hot fudge or strawberry sauce. Concoctions like the Strawberry Street Car Sundae, Firehouse Dalmatian Mint Sundae, or the Chocolate Chip Hot Fudge Sundae will make the guys and girls of today happy. So will the many kinds of ice cream floats and Coke products.

Jolly Holiday Bakery Café

APD: Yes, Cost: $
TYPE: American, Quick Service, Mobile Orders; Breakfast, Lunch, Dinner

The theme is Mary Poppins, the mood is casual, and the food is fine. For breakfast, there isn't a lot on offer, but there's a special grilled three-cheese sandwich with crispy bacon and black-berry jam that's very good. They've added an egg and bacon croissant and one with served with fruit. Several muffins and coffee are the main menu items, and there's the occasional quiche, but you can get cookies and desserts, too, if it doesn't strike you as a tad too early in the day for crème brûlée or cheesecake. For lunch (served after 10:30 a.m.), there's that nice toasted cheese sandwich paired with chips in addition to sandwiches like Caprese, roast beef, artisan BLT, turkey, and seasonally an appealing chicken-Waldorf on brioche with house-made chips. Salads like veggie, grilled chicken, and Jolly Holiday (lots of goodies including pecans, craisins, and a raspberry vinaigrette) are available and seasonal soups are, too. Kids can opt for a turkey sandwich Disney Check meal or the kids' mac and cheese. Desserts are the same as those available at breakfast. Dinner menu has the same items as lunch. It's a pretty little cafeteria with light, airy décor in shades of yellow and white. Look for the penguin waiters from the film in the stained glass windows. Sit outside under shady, striped umbrellas or on covered patios. The personal mini-bundt cakes aren't merely adorable, they're delicious. Not everyone likes the flavor of the Mickey rose-raspberry macaron with gold stripe (personally, I've *never* understood the appeal of a maca-ron), but if you haven't tried the moist coconut and white choc-olate snow-packed Matterhorn *macaroon*, save room! A mighty big difference exists between a macaron and a macaroon—not merely that extra "o." There's a lot to like at Jolly Holiday.

Market House

APD: Yes, Cost: $
TYPE: American, Quick Service; Breakfast, Lunch, Dinner

About halfway down Main Street on the right as you face the castle, you'll find this quaint shop that has any of your on-the-go breakfast needs well covered. Croissants, sandwiches, and a cage-free egg white wrap can be made with ham, eggs, sausage, cheese, spinach, and other choices. There is an extensively broad list of breakfast pastries, enough to please just about anyone, and Starbucks coffee is on the menu, along with frapppuccinos, smoothies, juices, teas, and milk. In addition to breakfast, you can always pop in for a treat at any time of day. Brownies, cookies, and the famously popular vanilla bean whoopie pie might be just what you need if your energy's fading fast. Don't get the mistaken idea that the Market House only offers sugary snacks, either. There's a serious effort to include a choice of fresh fruits, veggies, a fruit and yogurt parfait, and vegetarian fare, too. One super snack to grab and go is the pretzels, cheese, grapes, and carrot pack.

Plaza Inn

APD: Yes, Cost: $$-$$$
TYPE: American, Buffet/Family Style; Breakfast (Character Meal), Lunch, Dinner

The Plaza Inn has been a beloved fixture on Main Street ever since the park opened. For the first ten years, it was called The Red Wagon Inn, however, and was the nicest dining option in the park. For lots of guests, the tradition of dining here is essential on any visit to Disneyland. Food is plentiful and hearty with enough traditional choices to please most. Disneyland cast members dine in a cafeteria just behind the restaurant in a little place cleverly called the Inn Between.

Come for breakfast and you never know *who* you'll see at your table! It's called "Minnie & Friends—Breakfast in the Park." The "friends" will vary, and character meals never guarantee which ones will attend. Some of those may be Winnie the Pooh, Tigger, Eeyore, Piglet, Chip 'n' Dale, Cinderella's Fairy Godmother, Captain Hook, and other assorted characters. The buffet is substantial. Look for those ever-popular Mickey waffles, eggs, breakfast meats, fruits, cereals, pastries, French toast, made-to-order omelettes, and a wide selection of coffee, milk, juices, and more. The characters will come to your table, visit and pose for photos, and sign autographs. This is a real time-saver, since you'll see many favorite characters with no standing in line or elbowing in a crowd for their attention. Come early and be sure to make reservations for breakfast.

Lunch and dinner share the same menu and are also priced the same. The menu is tried and true, one that's been perfected over decades. People absolutely love the 3-piece fried chicken meal with a buttermilk biscuit, mashed potatoes, and vegetables. Another long-time favorite is the savory pot roast meal. Newer additions are pineapple-chipotle glazed salmon, penne with marinara or chicken pesto Alfredo, and a house or chopped salad. Kids can opt for a baked chicken leg meal or Disney check meal of penne with marinara, carrots, and applesauce. Desserts vary seasonally, and there are many beverage choices. No reservations are taken for lunch and dinner. You can dine inside or out. Tables outside have pretty, pink umbrellas and wrought-iron white chairs, perfect decor for the early 1900s, and you'll have a view of the entrance to Tomorrowland, the castle, and any parades that happen to be passing while you dine.

Refreshment Corner

APD: Yes, Cost: $
TYPE: American, Quick Service, Mobile Orders; Lunch, Dinner

At the very end of the street on your left as you head for Adventureland, there's a bright spot for quick, popular park food. Look for the red and white paneled umbrellas on the tables adjacent to the corner restaurant. Old-time piano tunes can frequently be heard plinking on the breeze as a pianist provides lively music for diners and passers by. Order all-beef hot dogs, mac and cheese dogs, chili cheese dogs, chili topped with cheese served in a sourdough bread bowl, a turkey dog kid's meal, or a Disney check meal with a yogurt smoothie, banana, carrots, and apple slices. You can also pick up Mickey pretzels or cheese-stuffed pretzels here, and simple desserts. The hot dogs come with either chips or apple slices. It's a nice, outdoor spot to people-watch. The food is relatively inexpensive, and the atmosphere is "frankly" fun.

CHAPTER THREE

Adventureland and New Orleans Square

Turn left at the end of Main Street U.S.A., and you'll quickly discover you're no longer in quaint, turn-of-the-century, small town America. You'll know because you'll find yourself in the lush jungles of the Africa, India, and Asia where poles are carved, roofs are thatched, and sounds are decidedly exotic. You may hear the faint roaring of the lion pride, raucous cries of toucans and parrots, and the snap of a crocodile's jaws. You're very definitely not in Marceline, Missouri, any more!

Cross under the sign spanning the entrance to this land of adventure and you'll see two gigantic faux elephant tusks on display behind a rather foreboding mask. Even some of the wood here is faux including the gigantic banyan tree, faux being a fancy French way of saying "not real," but the illusion is still masterful. When Walt Disney's park opened back in 1955, the Jungle Cruise was his favorite ride, one of the original seventeen. There had been some thought briefly given to housing live animals on the banks of the river, but the difficulties posed to guests from actual crocodiles, lions, elephants, gorillas, and hippos, cute yet in reality the most dangerous animals on the river, were soon abandoned in favor of less messy and dangerous stationary inhabitants that could be repainted when necessary. Like most of the country, Walt was a big fan of *The African Queen*, a 1951 film staring Humphrey Bogart and Katherine Hepburn. He envisioned a jungle cruise along those lines, serious and fraught with danger.

Some time after the park opened, he overheard a mother tell her son they didn't need to go on the Jungle Cruise again since they had already seen it before. He needed to think of a way to keep the attraction fresh and ever-changing. Hence came the lively spiels full of humor and wit, routines that quickly became legendary, from those lovable rogues who piloted the boats. Disneyland attractions should never grow stale but continue to grow and change so that every visit provided new things to experience. That was Walt's philosophy, and it's equally true today. You'd hardly recognize the Adventureland of those early days.

Two years after the popular *Swiss Family Robinson* came out in 1960, the entire, elaborate three-story tree house was dismantled from the set and brought to the park to provide a walk-through climb up and down the big banyan glimpsing the rooms and props actually used on location by young Moochie, who played Francis, and his family. By 1999, the Swiss Family set had retired to Florida and is now in residence at the Magic Kingdom in Walt Disney World. The Disneyland attraction was transformed into Tarzan's Treehouse in 1999.

The very first use of audio-animatronics, albeit with parrots and cockatoos, happened right here in Adventureland when the Enchanted Tiki Room was unveiled in 1963, a musical island paradise "where the birds sing words and the flowers croon, in the Tiki-Tiki-Tiki-Tiki-Tiki Room!" The unforgettable music was composed by the famous Sherman brothers. There was even a tropical rainstorm and dancing fountain!

Indiana Jones burst onto the Adventureland scene in 1995 with a rollicking roller-coaster ride following his wildly spectacular film debut in *Indiana Jones and the Raiders of the Lost Ark* in 1981. Lots of thrills, realistic set décor, and a perilous trip through a cursed temple make this one of the most popular rides in the park. The mutually beneficial relationship between Disney and George Lucas continues to this day.

It won't be long before you'll get into the spirit of this wild place. Walt Disney said of Adventureland: "Here is adventure. Here is romance. Here is mystery. Tropical rivers—silently flowing into the unknown. The unbelievable splendor of exotic flowers...the eerie sound of the jungle...with eyes that are always watching. This is Adventureland." There's plenty to see and do here, but how about finding something to feed your hungry team of explorers?

Adventureland Kiosks, Wagons, and Carts

- This is a stand, technically, called the South Sea Island **Fruit Stand**. Look for it directly opposite the Jungle Cruise attraction. It's loaded with healthy snacks. Fresh watermelon, pineapple spears, mango slices, grapes, a berry bowl, apple slices with caramel dip, and strawberries with chocolate dip (seasonally) are available. Pickle spears, veggies with dip, and chips round out the menu. Lots of water choices like coconut, mineral, or plain Dasani join Coke products, juices and coffee to meet your beverage needs.

Bengal Barbecue

ADP: Yes, Cost: $
TYPE: American, Quick-Service, Mobile Orders; Snacks

Just past the fruit stand you'll find this handy, grab-and-go counter with lots of savory, protein-packed snacks to keep you going. It's known for great-tasting skewers—beef (hot and spicy or sweet), chicken, veggie, bacon-wrapped asparagus, and BBQ pork belly, but there's also a "specialty skewer" that varies with the season, so ask about that once you're at the counter. One item guests just can't get enough of are the huge, soft tiger tail breadsticks! Pair those with a skewer or two, a veggie and hummus trio, a rice plate, or crispy shrimp spring rolls, and you'll be able to postpone any nascent hunger pangs indefinitely. Plenty of drink choices here, too.

Tiki Juice Bar

ADP: No, Cost: $
TYPE: American, Quick-Service, Mobile Orders ; Snacks

This is it, the Mother Lode of Disneyland's famous Dole Whip! Look for a couple of long, snaking lines in busy seasons—now's the time to try the Mobile Order option to save wait-time. It's near the Tiki Room entrance. If you've never tried this treat straight from the Dole pineapple fields in Hawaii, this is the time. It's vegan and very low in calories, besides being delicious and satisfying, one of those rare guilt-free pleasures with its own cult following. Get it plain in a cup as soft serve or in a pineapple juice float—no matter how you try it, you may find yourself hooked, just like so many people who've gone before you. There are fresh pineapple spears, as well as pineapple juice. See what's made Dole Whip a hit!

The Tropical Hideaway

ADP: No, Cost: $
TYPE: Vegetarian (also meat options), Quick-Service; Snacks

Located outdoors near the Jungle Cruise dock, you'll feel like you really are sitting at a table in the jungle, especially when Rosita, one of the birds who has apparently flown the coop from the Enchanted Tiki Room, starts entertaining the guests. This hideaway has wonderful baos, flat steamed dough wrapped around different types of filling to make neat little bundles of goodness you can hold in your hand. Here you'll find baos in spiced vegetable, gulgogi beef or lime chicken varieties. A chilled shaker of ramen noodels and fresh veggies with cashews and an Asian vinaigrette dressing is a good side dish, and there are pineapple spears, chips, whole fruit, mango slices, and watermelon to boot. If you have never tried the sweet treat known as "sweet lumpia," it's a wildly popular Malaysian delight—cream cheese and pineapple wrapped in wonton and fried, accompanied by Dole pineapple dipping sauce. It a word, it's oh-my-so-good...well, that's four words, but *don't* miss it. You can also get the famous Dole whip float, pineapple and orange swirl, a "loaded" whip (with exotic fruit and a crystallized hibiscus!) or a pineapple and raspberry swirl. Assorted bottled drinks go with the snacks. This is a fun place to stop with absolutely excellent snacks.

New Orleans Square

The grand dame of Disney's new "lands," the first one to be added after Disneyland opened, was called New Orleans Square. It isn't square in any sense of the word, however. There is no Town Square here, as there is on Main Street. The streets don't have square corners as they do in New Orleans, either. Last but not least, the jazz music here is about as far from square as you can get. This gorgeous new area, three acres, filled with winding streets and wrought iron balconies was unveiled in July of 1966 with great fanfare. Walt himself and the mayor of New Orleans, Louisiana, attended the ceremonies. It would be Walt's last major public appearance before his death in December of that year. At the opening, Walt joked that *his* New Orleans had cost more than the original Louisiana purchase—fifteen million dollars in 1803. The Disney version was built at a cost of eighteen million dollars, a staggering amount when just about ten years before the entire theme park had cost seventeen million to construct.

Walt and Lillian had a lot to do with envisioning this wonderful land. They designed plans for a private apartment on the second floor next to the entrance to Pirates of the Caribbean. Sadly, it was not to be, but you can still glance up to see the letters WD and RD for Walt and Roy worked into the wrought iron balustrade where the observation deck would have been. The couple chose most of the items stocked in the old One-of-a-Kind Shop from their many travels to distant parts of the world. Lillian, especially, worked very closely with the designer of the original Club 33, Emil Kuri, to put her personal stamp on the elegant décor there. The walls were covered with original artists conceptual sketches of the park. She and Walt hand-picked the lovely antiques on display at the club, many from the original French Quarter in Louisiana. Be sure to look for the doorbell and the number 33, for 33 Royal Street, immediately to your left as you exit Pirates. Don't bother pushing it, however. Only the lucky few with a highly selective membership are allowed access. When Disneyland sold no alcohol at all to the general public, libations always flowed liberally for members at the exclusive club!

The ever-popular Pirates of the Caribbean attraction was the last one to benefit from Walt's personal involvement. Three month's after his passing, it opened in 1967 and, with significant upgrades following the film franchise that began in 2003 with *The Curse of the Black Pearl,* continues to retain its place among the most successful of Disneyland attractions. Johnny Depp's appearance on the scene catapulted it into the twenty-first century and gave it relevance for an entirely new generation of young fans, many of whom are under the mistaken impression that the ride was based on the film instead of the other way around. Inside the attraction, you'll find the original theme restaurant. The Blue Bayou opened on the same day as Pirates and has been a beloved fixture of the Disney dining scene ever since.

Instant landscaping was added when the city of Los Angeles was in the process of renovating Pershing Square Park. Landscaper "Bell" Evans purchased seven enormous ficus trees so tall their tops were trimmed to fit beneath the overpasses and had them hauled down the 5 Freeway for replanting in New Orleans Square. The square looks out over the tall, white *Mark Twain* paddle-wheeler as it travels on the Rivers of America, and just past the shops or restaurants on the way to Critter Country stands the ante-bellum showplace known as the Haunted Mansion. Legend has it there are 999 Happy Haunts—and they're always looking for one more...

New Orleans Square Kiosks, Wagons, and Carts

- Near the central part of the New Orleans area, you'll find a **Churro Cart**. When Pirates celebrated its 50th anniversary, 16" long golden churros were available for a limited time. The line for churros was frequently longer than the line for the attraction!

- In front of the Mansion is a **Drink Stand** with flavored lemonade, frozen lemonade (this is delicious, believe me) in a souvenir sipper, substantial cinnamon rolls, hot chocolate in the cold months, and coffee with a souvenir mug available.

- This area boasts two **Ice Cream Carts**, one in the center of New Orleans and the other between Harbour Galley and Critter Country. Both have those yummy, super-popular premium Mickey ice cream bars, fruit bars, chocolate chip cookie ice cream sandwiches plus regular ice cream sandwiches, frozen bananas dipped in chocolate and nuts, Dibs (individual bites of candy-covered ice cream), cotton candy, and either regular or strawberry frozen lemonade. The frozen lemonade lasts a long time and isn't something that can be eaten in a hurry, so get it only when you've got a long walk ahead of you or plan to wait in a lengthy line for an attraction.

- A **Popcorn Cart** is located between the French Market and the Train Station. It sells those big, refillable souvenir buckets, premium buckets, regular-sized servings and Coke products.

French Market Restaurant

ADP: Yes, Cost: $
TYPE: American and Cajun-Creole, Quick-Service; Lunch, Dinner

Families enjoy the quick convenience of dining here, and the outdoor seating area shaded by awnings is beautiful. The food is presented cafeteria-style. You can watch boat traffic on the river, and there is often live Dixieland Jazz music played by the Royal Street Bachelors. Menus and prices are the same at lunch and dinner. Try Cajun-style meatloaf, a shrimp po' boy sandwich, jambalaya, or a jerk-spiced pulled pork sandwich if you want to feast Big Easy style. French dipped roast beef sandwiches, a generous helping a beef stew or creamy corn chowder presented in a boule (bread bowl), and lighter entrée salads might suit your preferences. Disney check meals are pasta and marinara or a chicken breast with rice. There is a kid's mac and cheese as well as a toddler-type mac and cheese meal. Desserts vary, but you can usually count of some stand-out decadent chocolate treat like a mousse cake, bananas Foster cheesecakes, plus a refreshing seasonal fruit plate. Non-alcoholic mint juleps, Coke products, tea, milk, hot chocolate, and Pirate's Punch round out the drinks menu. For a fast, filling, and tasty meal, the French Market is a consistently reliable option.

Mint Julep Bar

ADP: No, Cost: $
TYPE: American, Quick Service; Mobile Orders; Snacks

Sure, the refreshing lime-flavored, non-alcoholic mint juleps are pretty, even if they aren't everyone's cup of tea, but if you're in New Orleans Square, stop right here for the beignets! These warm, light, and airy donuts without holes come Mickey-shaped, either three or six to a bag, and are dusted with powdered sugar. Sometimes, a watermelon chili-lime variety is available and other flavors like butterscotch, pumpkin, or gingerbread are seasonal, but if you're just not sure, stick with the tried-and-true regular-flavored beignets that are gobbled up here at the rate of some 1.2 million per year. Beverages besides the juleps are on the menu such as coffee, tea, Coke products, juice, lemonade, and more. Look for this sweet little bar tucked into the French Market Restaurant's garden. If you didn't find a dessert to tempt you at the restaurant, give the fantastic beignets a try—you won't be disappointed (as long as you order the traditional flavored ones!).

Royal Street Veranda

ADP: Yes, Cost: $
TYPE: American, Quick Service, Mobile Orders; Snacks

Just beyond the entrance to Pirates of the Caribbean, you'll see this quaint, corner dining establishment. As you approach, look up to see the letters WD and RD for Walt Disney and Roy Disney entwined in the iron railing on the second story. They are far easier to notice, now that they are painted bright gold. Originally, they were quite well concealed among the green, decorative, iron swirls. The place is directly underneath where the planned family apartment was to have been built. If you or your group is fond of soup, this is your spot to refuel.

There are seasonal offerings like bacon, cheddar, and green onion fritters. Those big, sourdough bread boules come filled to the brim with either steak or veggie gumbo or a satiny-smooth clam chowder. It's reasonably priced, filling, and a lovely place to pause. Once you've finished the soup, if there's any room left for dessert, the Veranda has heavenly New Orleans fritters available. You'll have plenty of beverages choices to accompany your meal including the deliciously refreshing Jolly Roger Tea flavored with pineapple, orange, and mango.

Café Orleans

ADP: Yes, Cost: $$
TYPE: American, Cajun-Creole, Table Service; Lunch, Dinner

If this place looks familiar, that may be because it has been here since the beginning of New Orleans Square but was formerly called the Creole Café. Overlooking the Rivers of

America and just past the entrance to Pirates, look for this sweet, corner café that features real New Orleans specialties. Inside, the dark wood paneling and careful attention to detail takes you back to the nineteenth century. Dine inside or out on the patio under umbrellas.

Lunch and dinner menus and prices are the same. Look for seasonal specialties. Two starters are stand-outs, the tasty seafood gratin with lump crab, shrimp, and spinach, and the pommes frites (fries) tossed with garlic, Parmesan cheese, parsley, and spices. The fabulous Monte Cristo sandwich, based on France's Croque Monsieur, is one for the record books. If you haven't had it at Disneyland's New Orleans Square, do so now! Turkey, ham, and Swiss in a sandwich lightly battered and deep fried, perfectly complimented by a sprinkling of powdered sugar and a sweet berry purée. Vegetarians can order the 3-cheese option. Justifiably legendary, this entrée for many is absolutely *de riguer* when dining in the French Quarter. Other choices are nearly as good. The decadent lobster Cobb salad or Niçoise salad with ahi tuna is highly recommended, and there is a very nice steak and potato plate. Shrimp and cheese grits with sausage may be more of an acquired taste, as is the muffuletta chopped salad inspired by the many Portuguese settlers in New Orleans. Bourbon Street chicken offers diners authentic Southern flavors.

Maybe you want to split that Monte Cristo with your dining partner because you simply *must* save room for the sweet delights on display at this Café. The charming Mickey-shaped beignets come sided with dipping sauces, fruit coulis and house-made vanilla bean crème Anglaise. Toasted coconut flakes garnishing vanilla cake filled with coconut cream has the colorful panache of a Mardi Gras float; it will tantalize the most jaded of palettes. Sometimes, bananas Foster is on the menu, but if you're very fortunate, you'll be able to sample the ridiculously rich sourdough bread pudding with Praline-Chantilly crème, caramel sauce, and crumbles of praline brittle scattered over all. Oh, my, how challenging to choose just one!

Kids are kept happy with Disney check meals featuring steak, chicken, or sustainable fish. On the kids menu is mac and cheese or shrimp and cheesy grits, too. They might stick with low-fat milk or opt instead for Tinker Bell or Pirate's Punch. If you're feeling nostalgic, order an Espresso prepared from the very same machine that served Walt Disney more than fifty years ago. The coffee here is Joffrey's, a perfectly rich accompaniment to your sinfully indulgent dessert.

The Blue Bayou

ADP: Yes, Cost: $$$
TYPE: Cajun/Creole, Unique/Themed Dining; Lunch, Dinner

Around the corner from the entrance to Pirate of the Caribbean, you'll see the modest entrance leading to one of the most beautiful restaurants anywhere, and not just among those on Disney properties. You *must* make advance reservations and can do so sixty days before you arrive. Note that Disney hotel guests are given priority. Request a table by the water. You'll lose yourself in the illusion of dining at twilight on a Louisiana bayou. Japanese paper lanterns hang suspended from an enormous tree draped with Spanish moss. Realistic fireflies bob up and down on the river banks, their lights blinking on and off just like the real thing. Frogs croaking, crickets chirping, nightbirds calling, a banjo plunking softly in the distance, and the rhythmic sound of lapping water will instantly de-stress you. You'll be surrounded by building facades worthy of a Hollywood movie set making the illusion of twilight outdoors seem positively uncanny. Clouds drift slowly by overhead as the first stars come out. Now, if only the food offered and the service provided were as brilliant as the décor.

The sandwich that made the Blue Bayou beloved is here only at lunch at this point in time. It's priced at $29 and includes a fruit skewer. (The same sublime Monte Cristo is on both the lunch *and* dinner menu at the Café Orleans for $21, albeit without the fruit skewer.) The two restaurants share a kitchen, so you called always try pleading with the wait staff to see if one might be delivered to your table at dinnertime, but don't count on it. Other than the absence of the best sandwich ever at dinner, the lunch and dinner menus are practically identical and include catch of the day at $43, lamb at $44, bone-in rib eye at $48, and other entrées like portobello mushroom and rice, pork loin, salmon, chicken, and a somewhat tongue-in-cheek "surf and turf" combo at $52 that is currently only served at dinner. A house salad is included.

Kids can choose a fish or chicken Disney check meal. Mac and cheese or beef are on the regular kids menu. Desserts often include key lime tart, hazelnut chocolate cake, the Royal Street praline bundt cake, and crème brûlée. For the price, many diners expect the food to be prepared a bit more carefully and imaginatively. The kitchen is actually located *under* the restaurant and food comes up by way of a dumbwaiter; some guests have complained of lukewarm lobster tails and too-chewy filets. There are considerable critiques about uneven or even poor service. Likewise, many guests don't feel they received sufficient value relative to cost. Some of the wait staff, perhaps well-meaning yet inept, appear to have had inadequate training. My personal recommendation is to come for lunch, ask to sit at a table on the water, order the Monte Cristo, enjoy the incredible ambience, and bring any gratuitous lack of competence on the part of your wait person to the attention of a supervisor if it should happen. At these prices, there is no reason to accept anything less than adequate service. The restaurant setting itself is perfection. Both value and service could certainly benefit from a second look by management.

CHAPTER FOUR

Critter Country, Frontierland, and Star Wars: Galaxy's Edge

The next new land added to Disneyland following New Orleans Square was called Bear Country, named after the Country Bear Jamboree attraction that opened in the spring of 1972. Long before that, however, it had been known as Indian Village. Native Americans showcased tribal dances and traditions, and there were Indian War Canoes available for guests to paddle around Tom Sawyer Island—with an "Indian Guide" at the helm. The four acre area opened a year after the park itself and was Indian Village until 1971 when the Native Americans employed as cast members went on strike asking for a raise in pay, at which point the area was redesigned to accommodate the audio-animatronic bear performers who worked for no salaries at all.

With the 1972 transformation came the Mile Long Bar, named for the optical illusion of infinite reflections produced when two mirrors are positioned opposite each other. A casual restaurant overlooking the river was called the Golden Bear and then became the Hungry Bear a few years later. Teddy Barra's Swingin' Arcade was added and the canoes were renamed Davy Crockett Canoes. It was only four acres and the big 1972 refurbishment was done for a cost of just eight million dollars, as opposed to the eighteen million dollar cost of New Orleans five years before.

Country music lost some of its mainstream popularity luster and the Country Bears show had run its course. The Jamboree finally closed for good in 2001 and departed for Walt Disney World in Florida. A new, highly popular attraction called Splash Mountain was added in 1989. It's a log flume ride, similar to many at amusement parks across the nation. This mountain, though, has a variety of "critters" performing songs and jokes, many of them recycled from the old America Sings attraction that had been housed in the former General Electric Carousel of Progress. The theme at Splash Mountain was inspired by a controversial Disney film released in 1946, *The Song of the South*, featuring Uncle Remus stories and a blend of live action and animation. It's the only Disney film never released for sale in its entirety and was protested at the time of its opening for a sanitized depiction of the antebellum South. At the time Splash opened, the entire area was renamed Critter Country, its third name and the one it retains.

Once the Country Bears departed entirely, a charming attraction, The Many Adventures of Winnie the Pooh, was added. The store in the area was changed from Ursus H. Bear's Wilderness Outpost to the Crocodile Mercantile and then to Pooh Corner in 1996. Over the years from 1956 through today, this small northwest corner of Disneyland has gone through several major theme changes, but no matter how the place has evolved, it's a shady spot to enjoy a respite from the rest of the park when you want to relax and regroup.

Critter Country Kiosks, Wagons, and Carts

- Down by the river on your way to the Hungry Bear restaurant, you'll encounter a **Churro Cart**. They're 16 inches of warm, sugary goodness, and Disneyland is known for bringing out all sorts of different churro flavors, so check to see what the latest on offer might be. There are lots of churro carts, and they all sell beverages.

- Follow the path leading to Critter Country to find a **Fresh Fruit** stand well-stocked with a wide array of healthful options. Expect to find fruit selections like watermelon, mango, grapes, and pineapple, in addition to hummus, veggies and dip, juices, chips, beverages, apple crisps, a berry bowl, and apple slices with caramel.

- Across from Winnie the Pooh you'll see an **Ice Cream Cart**, just the thing on a warm, California afternoon. All your favorites are on hand, from Mickey bars to ice cream sand-wiches to Coke products and lots more.

- Technically, it's a store and not a kiosk, wagon, or cart, but it's worth mentioning the fun, fully-stocked store called **Pooh Corner** because inside you'll find those amazing marshmallow wands dubbed Tigger Tails, four marsh-mallows covered in caramel, dipped in orange candy coat-ing, sprinkled in neon-orange sanding sugar, and graced with black stripes just like Tigger's real tail. Haven't tried one? Now's your opportunity! You'll often see Cheshire Cat Tails here, too, in pretty purple and pink, as well as an extensive display of caramel apples, fudge, and seasonal confections created by Disney's talented in-house candy makers. The store itself is adorable and the merchandise, both edible and otherwise, is very special. Look for this shop near the exit to Splash Mountain.

Harbour Galley

ADP: Yes, Cost: $
TYPE: American, Quick Service, Mobile Orders; Lunch, Dinner

As you head into Critter Country, look to your right along the river and you'll see this little place on the dock where you and the gang can stock up on those tremendously tasty and much sought-after fresh lobster rolls! They come with house-made chips and are a relative bargain at under fifteen dollars. Try the yummy lobster mac and cheese or lobster galley chips for two more ways to satisfy your lobster cravings. Seasonally, you may find lobster pot pie soup on the menu. Cheddar broccoli soup and clam chowder are available in those big, sourdough bread bowls, but there are more seasonal soups that rotate on the menu. Lighter appetites will appreciate the shrimp salad, tuna salad sandwich, and a fisherman's salad with tuna, hard-boiled egg, olives, green beans, tomatoes, and onions. Side orders of fresh cut fruit will pair well with the options, and kids can order a Disney check meal with a Dannon smoothie, apple slices, a small banana, carrots, and low-fat milk. An assortment of beverages is available. There is a tremendous assortment of allergy-free and allergy-friendly choices here, so look for them or ask.

Hungry Bear Restaurant

ADP: Yes, Cost: $
TYPE: American, Quick Service, Mobile Orders; Lunch, Dinner

If you want a quiet, leafy-green place for lunch or dinner or just a snack, this is a wonderful place to pause. The covered outdoor pavilion overlooks the Rivers of America in rustic-chic style.

The trend in recent years is to make healthy choices possible, even when enjoying a day at Disneyland. The menu at Hungry Bear reflects this laudable effort. Yes, there are cheeseburgers and a zesty slaw or fries, along with crispy fried fish sandwiches, crispy chicken sandwiches, and chili-cheeseburgers, too, but you'll often find a Caesar turkey wrap and a really nice, fresh Picnic Salad that includes roasted, seasoned turkey, jicama, strawberries, craisins, and almonds on mixed greens with a light, strawberry vinaigrette dressing. This choice illustrates a serious turnabout on the part of Disney to accommodate a wider range of menu options. In addition, there are almost always allergy-free and/or vegetarian foods available, so don't hesitate to ask.

The Dannon smoothie Disney check meal is a good pick for kids. It's joined by kids meals like chicken nuggets and a hamburger. Toddlers may opt for their own Yummy Cheesy Macaroni. Hungry Bear is a place to indulge your sweet tooth! Funnel cake, milk and honey funnel cake (Winnie the Pooh would definitely order this one), a churro funnel cake—all house-made—are joined by a strawberry fruit bar or an ice cream sandwich made with chocolate chip cookies.

Frontierland

In the 1950s, the country was undergoing a huge Western renaissance. Television shows featuring rugged tales of the Wild West were all the rage. Walt Disney joined in from 1954-55 with five episodic stories of Davy Crockett staring Fess Parker and his sidekick Georgie Russell, played by Buddy Ebson. Little ones wanted coonskin caps and knew the theme song by heart, the one that started out "Born on a mountaintop in Tennessee..." The hit show tied in perfectly with the

1955 opening of Disneyland, and Fess and Buddy, decked out in costume and galloping in on horseback, helped launch the park on a live television program.

As the stockade gates to Frontierland opened, Ronald Reagan announced the event and Art Linkletter, Walt's very good friend, took over to interview the nation's most beloved frontiersman. A wagon train, rifle-toting cowboys, and cast members in Western dress treated the first visitors to a trip back in time. Walt Disney read the dedication to the viewing public:

> Here we experience the story of our country's past...the colorful drama of Frontier America in the exciting days of the covered wagon and the stage coach...the advent of the railroad...and the romantic riverboat. Frontierland is a tribute to the faith, courage and ingenuity of the pioneers who blazed the trails across America.

Today, history is seen a bit differently than it was all those decades ago. As sensibilities change, do does Disneyland. The burning cabin display on Tom Sawyer Island that had a settler out front, face-down with an arrow in his back, is no longer there. Early stage coach rides through the Painted Desert were prone to accidents, so they were likewise removed. The old Rainbow Ridge Pack Mule rides gave way to Big Thunder Mountain Railroad, lots more thrills and fewer spills, since the mules were apt to balk or even, on a few memorable occasions, roll with guests still in the saddle! Authentic Native American dancers gave way to Critter Country. Nevertheless, there's still a nostalgia for bygone days to be found in the area.

Ride the *Mark Twain* or the *Columbia* on a tour around the island. With just a little bit of imagination, you can visualize what the country looked like a century ago. The Golden Horseshoe Revue opened with a Western-style stage show that set the record for the longest-running musical show with more than 39,000 performances. Walt and his wife celebrated their thirtieth anniversary here in 1955 with a private party on July 13 shortly before the park opened to the public. Before having dinner and enjoying the show, he and Lillian ushered their guests aboard the *Mark Twain* for a cruise. Harper Goff, the same set designer who created Main Street, U.S.A., based his design for the Golden Horseshoe on a film he had done, *Calamity Jane* starring Doris Day, except that it was built to 5/8 scale.

These days, the two big boats still circle the island, kids explore Fort Wilderness and the caves on Tom Sawyer Island, refurbished and renamed Pirate's Lair in 2007, live shows happen at the Horseshoe, the shooting gallery lets sharpshooters test their skills, and at certain times of the season, you can still paddle one of the old canoes for yourself out on the Rivers of America. Just like the rest of the park, change has come to Frontierland, yet it manages to retain many of the elements that endeared the stories of his boyhood to Walt Disney. Regardless of the changes, the drama, excitement, and romance of life on the frontier can still be found right here on the other side of the tall log gates at the old stockade.

Adventureland Kiosks, Wagons, and Carts

- Churros are one of the most popular treats of all, and Frontierland has you covered right in front of the Golden Horseshoe. Disneyland is known for creating new "twists" on the old favorite flavor, so check the menu for any new ones you'd like to try. The **Churro Cart** sells icy, thirst-quenching beverages in addition to the warm churros.

- **Popcorn** is warm and fragrant and waiting for you on the river in front of the River Belle Terrace. Get a single serving or indulge in a big souvenir bucket. Coke products are sold.

- One of the perennial favorite snacks at the park is the **Mickey Pretzel**. It's generously sized, soft, and studded with big pieces of tangy salt—all that *and* it looks like your favorite mouse! Get one plain, stuffed with cream cheese, or with cheese dipping sauce. Monster beverages and Coke products can be bought at the pretzel cart.

- You've probably heard the rumor, traced to the actor who played Flynn Rider in *Tangled*. Zachary Levi told the public on late-night television that these smoky, enormous, juicy legs were actually the legs of Australian emus. Well, no. They are Tom turkey legs, and are about a pound and half of portable goodness. A

Jumbo Turkey Leg stand is set up near the River Boat Landing. There are lots more choices at the stand as well—chimichangas, corn on the cob, dried fruits, veggies, dip, hummus, chips, Coke beverages, fresh fruit, and that irresistibly perfect frozen lemonade at the Ship to Shore Marketplace near Thunder Mountain Railroad.

The Golden Horseshoe

ADP: Yes, Cost: $
TYPE: American, Quick Service, Mobile Orders; Lunch, Dinner

A fixture on the Frontierland scene from the very beginning, this saloon-style theatre boasts old-style Western décor. Check out all the mounted bulls' horns, chosen expressly by Walt himself. Chow down on some satisfying grub while taking in an entertaining show. The food is strictly secondary and there isn't a wide selection, but if you want to take a break and have some fun with your meal, this is the place to do it.

Items such as chicken wings, fish and chips, pepper jack chili mac, loaded potato skins, or a crispy chicken mixed green salad are available—standard park food served quickly to a large audience in a big hurry. Kids can choose chicken sliders or the Disney check power pack (yogurt smoothie, carrots, apples, banana, goldfish crackers, with low-fat milk or juice).

Desserts are a little bit more interesting than the meals here. There's an old-fashioned Coke float, a chocolate chunk cookie sundae, or a Dynamite Sundae with brownie, all fun and refreshing. A variety of beverages are served. Come for the show, don't expect a lot of variety on the limited menu, but order one of the special ice cream treats if you need a fast pick-me-up.

Rancho del Zocalo Restaurante

ADP: Yes, Cost: $
TYPE: Mexican/American, Quick Service; Lunch, Dinner

Mexican food has long been a part of Frontierland cuisine. Casa de Fritos (endorsed by the Frito Kid) from 1955 until 1982 where you could score a combo plate for ninety-five cents, Casa Mexicana from then until 2002, and now Rancho del Zocalo—the names have changed over the years, along with the prices, but the idea is similar. The zocalo in a Mexican town is the central square. You sit outdoors on a covered patio and fill up the troops with tasty, authentic Mexican specialties while watching the rest of the world go by. Breakfast has been served here in the past, and it was possible to order Mickey pancakes with sausage and scrambled eggs, but currently only lunch and dinner meals are available. Breakfast has been moved over to the Red Rose Taverne in Fantasyland, so get your Mickey pancakes there!

For lunch and dinner, ten traditional entrées are offered, along with three salads, and sides of chips. The trio of street tacos, beef/chicken/pork carnitas, sided with rice and beans is a sure-fire winner! Shrimp tacos, chilequiles, burritos, or enchiladas are filling, but if you're seriously hungry, go for the half-chicken. It's marinated in a complex blend of citrus and cumin with cilantro, fire-grilled, and served with rice and beans. The big carne asada and red chili enchilada platter is another crowd-pleaser with succulent beef and two cheese enchiladas plus rice and beans. Chicken tostada, beef tostada, and chicken Caesar salads offer pleasing options for lighter appetites.

Kids Disney check meals are a bean and cheese burrito or a chicken taco meal, and for the toddlers, order arroz con pollo or arroz con frijoles (chicken with rice or with beans). A veggie option is available with only beans and rice. Desserts are strictly traditional here: Mexican flan (custard), a fresh fruit cup, or cinnamon crips. Coke fountain beverages are sold, and there is a selection of coffee, tea, milk, juice, and hot cocoa seasonally. For fast, fresh Mexican specialties, look no further than Zocalo.

River Belle Terrace
ADP: Yes, Cost: $$
TYPE: American, Casual Dining; Breakfast, Lunch, Dinner

Take a table under a shady umbrella by the river, sit down and relax, as you select your meal from a wide variety of tasty choices. The fare is Southern-style with an emphasis on barbecue. This place has been busy for decades and remains a fan favorite for a very good reason—the food is good and the service is, too.

Breakfast is served during busy seasons only. The short rib skillet is delicious with sunny-side-up eggs, potatoes, and Texas toast. There's a bone-in pork chop, country biscuits and gravy, fried green tomatoes, bacon or sausage and eggs, and Mickey pancakes. The sweet skillet features monkey bread. Disney check meal for kids is oats with mixed berries.

For lunch or dinner, start with the yummy grilled and then chilled shrimp or a house salad with the works from craisins and fresh apples to gorgonzola cheese and candied pecans. There's pimento cheese dip with toasted bread or celery, a Southern tradition. If you'd like a big salad for your meal, there are two good choices, the popular chopped salad, lots of veggies and two kinds of beans plus corn, or a Terrace Wedge, the old-fashioned iceberg wedge with bacon and the house creamy buttermilk-Gorgonzola dressing. Both come with your choice of grilled/chilled shrimp, chicken, beef brisket, or BBQ tofu. There are vegetarian options at most places in the park. The rest of the entrées are definitely not light, but they're *big* on flavor. Beef or pork ribs—large portions, half a chicken, pulled pork sandwiches, fried chicken sandwiches, BBQ tofu, and fish are accompanied by sides like mashed potatoes, baked beans, seasonal vegetables, and more. The brisket sandwich is flavorful and tender with seasoned tater bites or seasonal veggies. Other sandwiches are a fried chicken or pulled pork.

Hope you've saved some room, since the Belle is known for turning out some pretty spectacular desserts. Who could resist her sticky pecan maple bourbon cake with brown sugar crème Anglaise and cranberry compote? It's a winner! If apple cobbler's more to your liking, there's one with Chantilly crème and a sweet biscuit topping. At times, monkey bread is offered. Seasonal parfaits may be all you can manage after the scrumptious meal, however. Kids Disney check meals are roasted chicken or fish or they can choose from ribs or mac and cheese on the kids menu. Coffee, tea, milk, and Coke products are your beverage options. This is a lovely spot with plenty of delicious food and the river view is simply gorgeous. Think about booking reservations for the Fantasmic! Dining Package for the perfect vantage point to see the show. It's the only venue in Disneyland where you can actually sit and eat dinner while you're watching.

Stage Door Café

ADP: Yes, Cost: $
TYPE: American, Quick Service, Mobile Orders; Lunch, Dinner

This little counter is tucked in beside the Golden Horseshoe. It's a quick way to grab and go if you're in a hurry. Options here are few. The hand-dipped corn dog is outstanding! Chicken nuggets, chicken fried steak sandwich, a grilled chicken spinach wrap, or fish and chips are the other items on the menu. All of them come sided with French fries or apple slices and dipping sauce.

Kids can count on the Disney check Dannon smoothie meal with a small banana, apple slices, carrots, goldfish crackers, and low-fat milk. The kids menu has a chicken slider or sometimes chicken nuggets. If something sweet would hit the spot, try a house-made funnel cake with strawberry, chocolate brownie, or powdered sugar on top or sometimes (if you're lucky) a Southern spicy peanut brittle. Beverages like Coke products, coffee, tea, chocolate milk, and water are available.

Star Wars: Galaxy's Edge

What is Star Wars: Galaxy's Edge doing north of Frontierland next to Critter Country, you might well ask? The answer: That's where they managed to find room! This was the old location of Big Thunder Ranch, formerly the Circle D, where generations of Disneyland horses, ponies, and mules were stabled. Various administrative buildings and warehouses were also relocated to make space. It meant a redesign of the railroad route and modification of the Rivers of America. Guests may access it by way of either Frontierland, Critter Country, or Fantasyland. It's fourteen acres of futuristic fun and space-age shenanigans for the whole family.

Plans were announced in August of 2015 and excitement among fans began building immediately. Construction began April 13, 2016. The Disneyland version opened in May of 2019 with the Walt Disney World counterpart's opening set for August 2019. When Bob Iger announced it, he said, the new land would be "occupied by many inhabitants: humanoids, aliens, and droids...the attractions, the entertainment, everything we create will be part of our storytelling. Nothing will be out of character or stray from the mythology." Since Lucasfilm had a hand in the design, rest assured things are amazing!

The planet depicted is Batuu, while the area itself represents a trading port during the time of the rise of both the First Order and the Resistance. One of the major attractions allows guests to "drive" the Millennium Falcon on a simulated secret mission called Smuggler's Run. A full-sized replica of the famous ship is part of the set. Start Wars: Rise of the Resistance includes several hundred animated objects immersing riders in a battle between the Order and the Resistance fighters; it is the largest dark ride ever built by Disney.

Guests are able to drink and dine in Oga's famous cantina, complete with music by the droid R-3X who acts as DJ. It is the first location at Disneyland to sell alcoholic beverages to the general public. The music for this newest land was composed by John Williams and recorded at Abbey Road Studios by the London Symphony Orchestra. Prepare to be immersed in a fantasy fictional realm that feels very real indeed.

StarWars: Galaxy's Edge
Kiosks, Wagons, and Carts

- In a few of the films, you've noticed Luke Skywalker sipping blue or green milk. Get yours at the **Milk Stand** and join the Resistance. It's frozen and refreshing.
- A **Popcorn Cart** is parked near Star Traders

Docking Bay 7 Food and Cargo
ADP: No, Cost: $
TYPE: American, Vegetarian, Quick Service, Mobile Orders; Breakfast, Lunch, Dinner

Everything looks "alien" at this large hangar serving galactic goodies. Sit indoors or outside, and you'll see evidence of the planet's crumbling infrastructure. The food calls to mind some of the out-of-this-world offerings available at the Animal Kingdom's Avatar region at Walt Disney World. Nothing will seem familiar, but that doesn't mean it won't be delicious. Breakfast is simple: Rising Moon Overnight Oats, a sweet roll called Mustafarian Lava Roll, and beverages. Lunch and dinner offer sticky pork ribs, marinated or crispy chicken, beef pot roast, chilled shrimp with noodles and a plant-based option called Felucian Garden Spread. Kids have two Disney check meals, a Yobshrimp Noodle Youngling Salad or A Taste of Takodana ("edible soil" that is actually black bean hummus and nuts with veggie chips and crisps). The regular kids menu has good old earth-friendly mac and cheese with crispy chicken and veggies—it's called Fried Endorian Tip Yip, but don't be dissuaded. The Oi-oi puff is a raspberry cream puff, while the Batuu-bon is chocolate cake with white chocolate mousse and coffee custard. The menu is limited, but more offerings should appear reasonably soon.

Kat Saka's Kettle

ADP: No, Cost: $
TYPE: American, Snack

Star Wars Fans know Kat Saka is a grain merchant. Find a warm colorful blend of Outpost Popcorn Mix that's filled with both sweet and spicy flavors sold here. It's perfect to munch on as you discover surprises in store at the Black Spire Outpost. Coke beverages are available.

Oga's Cantina

ADP: No, Cost: $
TYPE: American, Table Service, Unique/Theme Dining, Bars and Lounges; Lunch, Dinner

Just about anyone who has seen the Star Wars films has dreamed of stopping in at Oga's for a bite to eat and a libation. Try one of the brightly colored concoctions like the Jedi Mind Trick cocktail, Bad Motivator IPA, or Toniray wine, but if you order an alcoholic beverage, be sure you have your valid planet Earth ID available. Some drinks have boba balls, a fun addition that adds interest and color.

CHAPTER FIVE

Fantasyland, Mickey's Toontown, and Tomorrowland

The land Walt Disney always said was closest to his own heart, the one where children and adults are equally likely to discover their dreams can come true, is Fantasyland. On opening day, he said:

> Here is a land of imagination, hopes and dreams. In this timeless land of enchantment the age of chivalry, magic and make-believe are reborn and fairy tales come true. Fantasyland is dedicated to the young and the young at heart, to those who believe that when you wish upon a star your dreams do come true.

Back then, it was representative of a European Renaissance village. The antique King Arthur carousel was at its heart, surrounded by gentle rides with some darker shadows, too, because fairy tales, much like lives, are not all sweetness and light. There were the spinning tea cups at the Mad Tea Party, antique autos at Mr. Toad's Wild Ride, small pirate ships on Peter Pan's Flight, open boats on the Storybook Land Canals, and mine carts at Snow White's Scary Adventures, the "Scary" part not being added to the title until preschoolers became so frightened at the witch popping out at them that their parents clamored for a heads up!

In 1983, Fantasyland became *New* Fantasyland. The ambience morphed to a Bavarian village; extensive updates put a brand-new polish on the old and familiar. Many of the original attractions remain, but over the years this area has undergone significant changes and additions. The Matterhorn was built after 1959's *Third Man on the Mountain*, and its roller-coaster bobsleds have been among the park's most popular attractions ever since opening in June of that year. It's a Small World joined the park after the New York World's Fair in 1964-65. It's bright clock façade with characters coming out to chime the hours has become synonymous with the appeal of Disneyland to countries throughout the world. It's difficult to imagine Fantasyland without the carefully tended topiary gardens where landscaping comes to life outside the ride.

Other additions haven't made quite the splash that the Matterhorn or Small World did, but they've given children of all ages a chance to relive beloved memories and to make new ones. Dumbo the Flying Elephant, the Casey Jones Circus Train, Alice in Wonderland, Pinnochio's Daring Journey, and Tinker Bell's Pixie Hollow present familiar friends in their own special ways. Most things in Fantasyland trace their roots back to Disney films. Even the castle, iconic symbol of everything Disney, is a nod to the Sleeping Beauty castle from the 1959 film. The film was nearly a decade in production; preliminary work began in 1950. There was a walk-through diorama of the story early on, it was closed for a number of years for "security purposes" after 9/11, and it's now been reimagined and is open again.

Many guests could happily spend their entire day in Fantasyland, and regardless of whether that's you or you're just passing through, you are sure to need some refueling stops along the way.

Fantasyland Kiosks, Wagons, and Carts

- Fantasyland has a dozen of these little snack stops, more than any other land! There are three **Churro Carts** here. One is behind the Matterhorn as you head towards Small World, a second one is just a bit farther on past Edelweiss, and the third is near Casey Jr. They have warm 16-inch-long churros and Coke products. Fantasyland alone has more churro carts than the entire Magic Kingdom at Walt Disney World!

- There are two **Drink Stands**, one near the Storybook Land Canal Boats and the other opposite the Village Haus Restaurant. When you want a beverage and a snack, you'll encounter all kinds of fresh fruit—whole, sliced, or with dipping sauce. Berry bowls are another health-conscious alternative to more sugary or calorie-laden treats. Veggies with hummus, chips, dried fruit, pickles, juices, Coke products, and other drinks are sold, too.

- Three **Ice Cream Carts** are vying for space in one land! There is one by Dumbo, one on the way to Small World, and one close to the Fantasyland Railroad Station. You'll find lots of frozen goodies to chose among like premium Mickey ice cream bars, Mickey ice cream sandwiches, chocolate chip cookie ice cream sandwiches, frozen fruit bars, frozen lemonade, Dibs, frozen bananas and more!

- On a little footpath that leads toward the castle on the left side of the central hub, **Maurice's Treats** are sold by Belle's father. The offerings, like the old gentleman himself, are a little bit eccentric. Don't pass up this chance to try The Grey Stuff—it's delicious! He also has a strawberry twist, and speaking of twists, how about a garlic cheddar bagel twist? Get dipping sauces in grey stuff, strawberry rose, or marinara. Other unusual items are the boysen-apple freeze (boysenberries are famous in California) or the red rose lemonade freeze.

- **Popcorn Carts** are located behind the Matterhorn under the Monorail track and opposite Small World.

- If you find yourself yearning for a hot, salt-studded Mickey pretzel, you'll find a **Pretzel Cart** on the way to Small World.

Edelweiss

ADP: No, Cost: $
TYPE: American/Mexican, Quick Service, Mobile Orders; Snack

While this place may be technically labeled a kiosk, it more of a casual counter-serve where you can sit for a casual meal next to the Matterhorn and listen to delighted screams emanating from the bobsleds as you eat! You'll know it by the big, gilt turkey on a sign sign suspended from a flowered hook out front, a holdover from days of yore when few people read but everyone could recognize a turkey, pretzel, or sheaf of wheat advertising the merchandise. That's because Edelweiss has those jumbo smoked turkey legs here, and there's corn on the cob, either buttered or chili-lime, to go with it. If that's too much, try chips and a chimichanga, a Mexican favorite snack. There are the usual assortment of Coke products, but if you're warm and tired, the frozen Fanta (another Mexican delight) in blue raspberry or cherry or a frozen apple juice will happily revive you.

Red Rose Taverne

ADP: Yes, Cost: $
TYPE: French/American, Quick Service, Mobile Orders; Breakfast, Lunch, Dinner

Pass the carousel, if you're walking through the castle from the hub, and turn left. Keep walking until you can go no farther without leaving Fantasyland and you'll find this quaint little taverne done in the French style. It's a quick and casual way to grab a meal on the go without spending much time.When it's available, the Croque Madame is a well-balanced breakfast of toast, an egg, tomatoes, lemon béchamel sauce, and a side of fresh fruit. This is the spot for wonderful Mickey-shaped pancakes served with fresh berries, a great choice for kids and adults alike. There is a veggie garden hash, a big breakfast platter (eggs, bacon, potatoes, and a croissant), regular buttermilk pancakes with bacon and eggs, and a breakfast-type flatbread.

Lunch and dinner offer similarly hearty entrées. This is a place where some careful thought and effort have gone into designing the appealing selections. For a taste sensation, and it's not always available, order the poutine or poutine flatbread, a Canadian favorite where gravy tops beef, fries, and cheese curds. The Beast's Angus burger with caramelized onions and Gruyère is a cut above average park fare. So is Lumiere's chicken sandwich with its apple slaw, onion bacon jam, and fried cherry peppers. Vegetarians might opt for the samosa (fried savory pastry) and cauliflower sandwich, which is actually a lot better than it sounds! There's a mozzarella flatbread and a couple of nice, light salads as well, one of them with chicken.

Disney check meals for kids are a carved turkey sandwich or the power pack meal (yogurt smoothie, carrots, apple slices, small banana, and goldfish crackers) or a cheese pizza, cheeseburger, or mac and cheese from the regular kid's menu.

Before you go, try the grey stuff gateau (that's cake in French)—it's delicious. As Lumiere says, "Don't believe me? Ask the dishes!" Yes, this is the place to see what all the fuss is about. After a very good meal, the light cookies and crème dessert with raspberry center and red velvet cake is just right. It may be grey, but it's incredibly tasty, not to mention beautifully decorated. There's sometimes a lemon mousse cake with strawberry rose filling, "rose" flavor being a decidedly odd choice for pairing with cake, and crispy treats. All sorts of traditional beverages are available, but if you want something a bit different, try Gaston's Famous Brew. The icy apple and mango punch topped with passion fruit foam is surprisingly good! Many guests make a special trip to the taverne just for this brew. It's a palpable hit!

Troubadour Tavern

ADP: Yes, Cost: $
TYPE: American, Quick Service; Snack

Practically anything on the menu here is appealing and tasty. It is located to the left of Small World on your way to Toontown. Look for the big, covered tent. There's plenty of room!

The tavern specializes in snacks, but you and your party can easily make a meal of it here.

A brat? Ho hum, but not when it's on a garlic and herb brioche bun with hickory-smoked bacon sauerkraut. A BBQ smoked turkey leg is on the menu, but only while supplies last! How about a loaded baked potato with all the fixin's—broccoli and cheese or sour cream and bacon. Pretzels with cheese sauce are kid pleasers, as is the souvenir refillable popcorn bucket. There's a power pack Disney check meal.

The cinnamon-apple "baton" is a stuffed portable pastry that it tastes like apple pie. A frozen lemonade/strawberry bar or Nibs, those bite sized ice cream treats covered in chocolate, fill in for dessert. Lots of beverages are available, but kids may want to try the special Enchanted Cherry-Apple Lemonade.

Mickey's Toontown

This small "land" with two attractions was inspired by 1988's *Who Framed Roger Rabbit?* The old Jolly Trolley closed in 2003 and is now on display only for photo ops. Take the path that runs to the left side of the Small World façade to find yourself in a world where cartoons rule the day and the scenery is reminiscent of 1930s Los Angeles. Mickey and Minnie Mouse have houses here, Donald docks his boat, Chip 'n' Dale have a treehouse, and Goofy's playhouse can also be found. The area has greater appeal for kids than for adults.

Roger Rabbit's Car Toon Spin and Gadget's Go Coaster tend to attract a decidedly younger crowd. Roger Rabbit allows riders some control over the taxi cabs as they are being pursued by weasels. It's three and a half minutes of spins and dips. There are some pretty scary-looking clowns, and it's dark and loud inside, so be aware if this might upset your young child. Gadget's "hollowed out acorn seats" are expressly designed for one child and one adult. The ride lasts one minute. There is often a wait for these attractions, and the "land" that seems like animation come to life is a perfect size and scale for younger visitors. They're free to explore all the cool spaces in a way that isn't possible in other parts of the park. Eating here is quick and definitely snack-style, just the way the 'toons prefer it!

Toontown Kiosks, Wagons, and Carts

- There's a **Frozen Beverage Stand** shaped like a darling little trailer just outside Goofy's playhouse where you can partake of frozen blue raspberry, wild cherry, or apple flavored frozen beverages. It is also stocked with bags of chips or cotton candy.

- Next to Goofy's Gas Station, you'll find the answer to eating healthy in Toontown! There's a **Fruit Stand** filled with whole or sliced fruit, dried fruit, berry bowls, pickles, veggies with hummus, and all sorts of drinks like low-fat milk and sugarless juices.

- An **Ice Cream Cart** is located on your way into Mickey's Toontown to the left side of the walking path. On a hot day, find Mickey's premium ice cream bars, ice cream sandwiches, and other frozen treats to keep you cool and comfy.

- The smell of warm, fresh **Popcorn** on the air ought to lead you right over to Chip 'n' Dale's Tree House. You can purchase Coke products, too.

Clarabelle's

ADP: Yes, Cost: $
TYPE: American, Quick Service; Snack, Lunch, Dinner

The busiest bovine in Toontown runs this little counter to the left of the bank. There are three "moo" plate specials, even if the kids—or even their parents—are too young to remember the days of blue plate specials, and luckily not *everything* is geared strictly for kids! Get the surprisingly nice slow-roasted turkey sandwich (no lunch meat at Clarabell's) with chips. There's a big fruit salad and a tasty chef's salad that adults will find appealing. The Disney check meal is the Power Pack (yogurt smoothie, sliced apples, carrots, small banana, whole grain goldfish crackers).

As you might imagine, Clarabelle's prominently features ice cream desserts, called "Utterly" Sweet Treats. Soft-serve frozen yogurt is a welcome treat at this counter under the black and white spotted awning. Toppings are on the menu, too! All the usual ice cream treats are sold like premium Mickey bars, ice cream sandwiches, frozen fruit bars, and all kinds of beverages are provided to accompany the snacks and treats.

Daisy's Diner

ADP: Yes, Cost: $
TYPE: American, Quick Service; Snack, Lunch, Dinner

Daisy has a counter featuring pizza, either cheese or pepperoni, adjacent to Clarabelle's. Beverages are sold to accompany your snack, and there are tables and places to sit under shady umbrellas nearby. Dining choices are limited but should satisfy many of the younger guests.

Pluto's Dog House

ADP: Yes, Cost: $
TYPE: American, Quick Service; Snack, Lunch, Dinner

Pluto sells—what else—hot dogs, of course! Get a premium hot dog with chips or sliced apples and a drink of your choice at this tiny stand shaped like a realistic dog house. The menu hangs inside on an oversized bone suspended from the ceiling. Bacon mac and cheese foot-long hot dogs or plain foot-longs are sold. Kids can get a Disney check turkey sandwich meal or a kid's turkey dog meal. Toddlers will find their favorite Yummy Cheesy Macaroni with a Go-Go squeeZ applesauce and low-fat milk. Pluto's is adjacent to Daisy's, so that all three little food counters line up in a row to the left side as you face the bank.

Tomorrowland

When it opened in 1955, this land was all sleek silver jumpsuits and futuristic hopefulness, accented by the tall Rocket to the Moon pointed toward space headed for a moon that was yet to be explored by humans. Autopia was open and the Astro Jets, and the train made a stop, but it was just a glimpse of what the land would eventually contain. Walt Disney observed of this land of things to come, "Tomorrow can be a wonderful age. Our scientists today are opening the doors of the Space Age to achievements that will benefit our children and generations to come. The Tomorrowland attractions have been designed to give you an opportunity to participate in adventures that are a living blueprint of our future." Like most predictions, some came true and a good many still haven't.

Speaking of scientists, Werner von Braun and other actual "rocket scientists" took part in the original design of this area as technical consultants. A major renovation introduced New Tomorrowland in 1967 as more attractions and exhibits were added. In 1998, designers stopped trying to stay a jump ahead of reality and decided instead to look at things through a Jules Verne lens, so the land of tomorrow became decidedly retro, colorful, and cool. The submarine voyage came and went as did a station for the now defunct Skyway—you can still see the two holes through which the little gondolas passed in the middle of the Matterhorn. Journey through Inner Space let you shrink to the size of an atom. The PeopleMover took you on an elevated track at two miles an hour with an overview of all the land had to offer. The wonderfully elegant House of the Future and the General Electric Carousel of Progress gave us hints of a world to come, a brighter tomorrow where people could benefit from the advances in technology. Eventually, many became commonplace—microwave ovens, electric toothbrushes, and phones that let you see who you're talking with have all come to pass. We may not be wearing silver jumpsuits or donning jet packs to get around, but a great many of the things introduced to the public in Tomorrowland turned out to be accurate predictions about the way we live today.

Today, Autopia is still going strong. The Monorail transports guests to Downtown Disney and the Disneyland Hotel and Resort. Space Mountain remains the biggest draw with the longest wait time. The Jets became the Astro Orbitor and Buzz Lightyear's Astro Blasters lets you feel like you've dropped right into a video game. Star Wars is well represented at Jedi Training: Trials of the Temple and by the ever-changing outcomes, randomly generated by computer, and at Star Tours—the Adventures Continue. You can meet your favorite Star Wars characters and see movie props in the Star Wars Launch Bay. Even the subs are up and running again, this time with a Finding Nemo reboot.

The original theme park, as Walt Disney imagined it, would be always changing, never finished. He said, "Disneyland will never be complete. It will continue to grown as long as there is imagination left in the world." That sentiment is especially evident in Tomorrowland.

Tomorrowland Kiosks, Wagons, and Carts

- You'll see a **Churro Cart** is located near the entrance to the Astro Orbitor if you are approaching it from the central hub. Get 'em while they're warm and covered in sugar and cinnamon, Mexican-style.

- Two **Drink Stands** have your beverage needs covered. One is near the entrance to Alien Pizza Planet, while the other is next to the Star Wars Launch Bay. All the typical drinks and Coke products are available, and one of them usually has frozen lemonade.

- An **Ice Cream Cart** between Autopia and the Monorail station sells premium Mickey ice cream bars, Mickey ice cream sandwiches, chocolate chip cookie ice cream sandwiches, strawberry bars, strawberry-lemonade bars, chocolate frozen bananas, and drinks.

- A **Popcorn Cart** can be found near Star Trader. That smell of fresh, hot popcorn is practically irresistible, either in a regular serving size or in a big, shareable, refillable souvenir bucket.

- **Pretzels** are soft, warm, and just waiting for you past the churro cart on your way to the Astro Orbitor from the hub. Like many of the food treats at Disneyland, they are shaped like Mickey's face. If you haven't had one, you'll discover they are surprisingly filling and delicious. One will easily hold you until your next meal.

Alien Pizza Planet

ADP: Yes, Cost: $
TYPE: American, Quick Service, Mobile Orders; Lunch, Dinner

This tasty Pizza Planet is between Space Mountain and Star Wars Launch Bay. Be sure to notice that retro-looking red and white rocket ship outside. It's a smaller, scaled down version of the huge TWA moonliner rocket that stood in Tomorrowland when the park first opened. At eighty feet tall, it stood even higher than the seventy-seven foot Sleeping Beauty's Castle. Eventually, the Matterhorn became the highest structure in the park at one hundred and forty-seven feet. Be sure to check out the history of the Tomorrowland as told through memorabilia on display at the restaurant.

At many restaurants in the park these days, there is little if any difference between lunch and dinner menus, and that's true here. Pizza is the main draw, and you can get it by the slice or whole with all the usual toppings. There's bowtie pasta, chicken fusilli, a veggie pasta dish, and a S'mores parfait. Salads like astro antipasto, nebula noodle with grilled chicken breast, and a centurion Caesar are lighter alternatives to pizza and pasta. The Disney check meal is "space-ghetti" with meatballs, and the kids menu offers cheese pizza. Toddlers may want the mac and cheese.

There are two fun desserts available currently, both featuring green aliens. Get them while they're here! The alien parfait is a delectable combination of cookies and cream, raspberry, and three white chocolate eyeballs plus a smile! Macarons aren't a personal favorite, but an exception has to be made for these happy, bright green faces held together with blackberry-flavored purple filling and lemon custard in the center. They look exactly like the irresistible Toy Story characters from space. A lot of menu items here claim to be "star" or "space" or "planetary," but the alien desserts really *are* out of this world!

Galactic Grill

ADP: Yes, Cost: $
TYPE: American, Quick Service, Mobile Orders; Breakfast, Lunch, Dinner, Late Night (only seasonally)

This enormous eatery is to the left if you enter Tomorrowland facing the Astro Orbitor. There are many tables under shady umbrellas and plenty of seating. The focus is on offering vegetarian choices and healthy options, but there's plenty to satisfy practically everyone. For breakfast, try the loaded breakfast sandwich, a breakfast burrito, French toast sticks, and fresh, seasonal fruit. Kids can get Disney check meals, either the breakfast slider with turkey bacon and egg on a bun sided with fresh fruit or the Power Pack breakfast with yogurt smoothie, grapes, carrot sticks, and small banana with low-fat milk. All the traditional breakfast beverages are available.

At lunch and dinner, there's an Angus burger or cheeseburger and a fried chicken sandwich, but you can also try a lighter chopped veggie salad or a veggie wrap served with either fries or a Greek yogurt. Disney check meals include a turkey sandwich or the Power Pack. Kids can also choose a mini-hamburger or chicken nuggets, and there is a toddler favorite, too, the yummy cheesy macaroni. There are a few dessert options like a Rice Krispie treat or Mickey ice cream bar, but it's nice to also find a seasonal parfait.

If you're planning to stay at the park until it closes, one innovative offering here at the Grill is a late night dining menu designed just for you. This is where things start to get interesting—the menu showcases some exciting new tastes, but only during busy seasons. Yes, please, to both the sweet star clusters and the spicy star clusters, crispy chicken bites served over blue cheese slaw with sauce (buffalo or sweet chili) in a waffle bowl with pickle chips. A souped-up quesadilla with pepper jack cheese and chipotle is sure to keep you awake. Loaded potato bites pair great with the micro burger sliders, both featuring caramelized onions. For those who've stayed so late they feel ready for breakfast, order the French toast little dippers with salted caramel and strawberry sauce, just the thing to revive dragging feet and drowsy eyes. The late night dining menu is a winner! It will change with the seasons, and it isn't always available, but it's fun to try different things, so prepare to be surprised.

CHAPTER SIX

Downtown Disney District

This twenty-acre, open-air shopping and dining area opened on January 12, 2001. It links Disneyland, Disney California Adventure, and the three resort hotels, Disneyland's Grand Californian Hotel & Spa, the Disneyland Hotel, and Disney's Paradise Pier Hotel. Spend at least $20 here to get three hours of parking or eat at one of the table service restaurants and get five free hours. Prices are $14 per hour after that and are subject to capacity. Lose your ticket and the cost is $56! There are currently about twenty-plus places to eat in the district, everything from a leisurely unique/themed dining experience at Catal to grabbing a pretzel on the go at Wetzel's. There's a Monorail station at Downtown Disney accessible from Disneyland, but riding it requires a valid park admission ticket.

Like any shopping area, tenants come and go, but the district overall always has a lot to offer. As long as you're at one of the theme parks, catch a ride on the Monorail from Disneyland to Downtown Disney or walk over from the theme parks and eat at one of the restaurants here. They offer widely expanded menu options from some of the more typical kinds of "park food," and there are creative cocktails, craft and bottled beers, and some exceptionally nice wines available with your meal, something you *won't* find in the theme parks unless you're a member of Club 33 or visiting the new Oga's Cantina in Star Wars: Galaxy's Edge.

It was announced that a new 700-room four diamond Disney hotel was set to open in 2022. It would have claimed seventeen acres of prime real estate in the Downtown Disney District and displaced current tenants Rainforest Café (now closed), ESPN Zone (now closed), Earl of Sandwich, as well as the AMC multi-plex theatres. Some of these hoped to return to open venues *inside* the new hotel, but that sucking sound you heard in October 2018 was the plug being pulled on construction of the new hotel.

Ballast Point Brewing Co.

ADP: Yes, Cost: $$
TYPE: American, Casual Dining, Bars and Lounges, Table Service; Lunch, Dinner

This is the only brewery, a three-barrel rig, operating at the resort. In addition to house-made offerings, you'll find plenty of other craft beers to choose from on tap. The ambience here is pure Californian. The décor is fresh and nautical. Seating is upstairs (elevator available) and you'll have a great view of the hustle and bustle of Downtown Disney as well as a behind-glass look at beer as it's being brewed.

Eat inside or on the patio—there are heaters if it gets chilly. Start your meal with one of the delicious "plates to share" like the popular duck confit nachos—if you think this isn't fabulous, think again, my friend. How about a few of those "Wahoo" beer steamed mussels with Serrano chili or maybe some of those addictive chicharrones (pork cracklings) with house-made pimento cheese, grilled bread, and pickles—yum. Classic salads like wedge or chopped Caesar come with the option of adding chicken or grilled fish. Flatbreads such as the fabulous "Black Marlin" (smoked ham hock) will certainly go well with a cold brew. If you haven't tried the veggie "impossible" burger, here's your chance. They call it that because it's practically impossible to tell it from the real thing. It's hard to beat the Baja fish tacos, sesame-crusted ahi tuna, or even good old beer-battered fish and chips.

A couple of desserts will fill you up while satisfying that sweet tooth, crème brûlée cheesecake or "Victory at Sea" S'mores, and the kids in your group will find chicken skewers, crispy fish, chicken tenders, corn tortilla quesadilla and plenty of fun sides like chips and avocado, fries, and healthful fresh carrots and apples.

Honestly, though, beer is the main event here, and you'll find it neatly divided into descriptive categories like rich and malty, crisp and bright, tart and sour, barrel aged, and more. If wine's more to your liking, no worries. Reds, rosés, and whites in abundance can be had, the majority from some of the best California vineyards but with some international options, too. Great food, great beer!

Catal

ADP: Yes, Cost: $$
TYPE: American/Mediterranean, Table Service, Fine/Signature Dining; Breakfast, Lunch, Dinner

A big cut above many other restaurants in the theme parks, Catal has food that impresses most diners; look elsewhere if you're looking for a bargain meal. Catalán is a region of Spain, yet the choices here are interpreted in fresh, new ways. Book a reservation to be safe because it's sometimes quite busy. If you aren't immediately shown upstairs and are seeking a more formal dining experience, ask to be seated there. There's a dining room as well as an alfresco terrace with a nice view. Downstairs is the more casual bar with a different menu and ambience. Some diners have complained about the service. As I've said, but it's worth repeating, in a Disney restaurant there is never a need to accept less than adequate service. Sometimes, you simply need to bring it to your server's attention. Sometimes, you need to speak with a manager. Regardless, don't wait until you are upset and angry. Be firm, be reasonable, and be polite.

There is nearly universal applause for the cuisine here, and justifiably so! At breakfast, you'll find lots of American favorites such as pancakes, omelettes including a "skinny" one, French toast, eggs, breakfast meats, and potatoes, but the choices don't stop there. Try the chiliquiles with eggs, chips, queso fresco (fresh cheese), guacamole and chorizo (spicy sausage). There's a tasty breakfast burrito filled with scrambled eggs, cheddar, bacon, potatoes, and covered with a mild red chili sauce. Looking to start out light? Get the breakfast bowl with Greek yogurt, honey, granola, and berries. There are mimosas, Buenos Días margaritas, California sparkling wines, and bloody Marys to accompany your selections. The non-alcoholic beverage menu is extensive and exciting—mango lemonade, Lavazza (from Italy) coffee, orange guava juice, and a strawberry banana smoothie are just a few. Kids are accommodated with their own appealing meal choices.

Lunch has a slightly abbreviated menu, although prices are nearly identical. Crispy calamari, bacon wrapped dates with blue cheese, or ahi bruschetta are stand-out starters. There are lots of delightful salads—almost twenty of them! Get yours with chicken, shrimp, hangar steak, prawns, or manchego cheese. The wedge salads are tasty, too, and done up with all the elements of a traditional wedge. Lunch entrées are steak, salmon, or a wonderful roasted chicken paella full of Bilbao sausage and peas over saffron rice. At $28, it's a lot for lunch in both price and size, but it's a great choice if you're hungry and want to try something in the Catal style. Sandwiches at lunch are burgers, rib, turkey, fish, and a really nice Cuban with shaved porchetta, Swiss cheese, mustard, and aioli. All of them are sided with Catal fries.

At dinner, the number of entrees jumps from three to eleven. Have you ever wanted to sample suckling pig? I'll give that a hard pass, but if you're undaunted, then go for it! The oxtail ragu (ragout) is inventive and many guests love the Divers scallops. Steaks here are offered in many ways. Be very careful about specifying *exactly* how you prefer yours done. There are some nice Australian lamb chops or sometimes pork chops as well as prime rib au jus. At dinner, there are currently four kinds of paella: seafood, suckling pig, lobster, or chicken. My, that's a lot to eat, and it would be no wonder if you find yourself too full for dessert, but it would also be a shame to pass it up at Catal.

Tres leches cake, chocolate chip bread pudding, and a triple chocolate mousse cake can be served with a few spoons so everyone can try a taste. Imaginative craft cocktails, craft and bottled beers of every kind, and a truly prodigious wine list, most from California but France, Spain, and Italy are also represented, will complement your every entrée here. Catal is a lovely choice for a leisurely, delicious meal in an old world setting, whether you're celebrating something special or simply wish to indulge in a memorable meal.

Catal Uva Bar

ADP: Yes, Cost: $S
TYPE: American/Mediterranean, Table Service; Breakfast, Lunch, Dinner

This is the downstairs section of Catal, a more casual bar area with an abbreviated menu and lots to offer. The three, tall martini glass sculptures set the mood at the circular outdoor bar. You'll feel like you've dropped right into the Jazz Age. Uva means grape in Spanish, and there are some forty wines available by the glass to accompany your tapas, small plates with a variety of tasty things to share. There are plenty of them. Give the corn arepas a try—corn cakes with pulled pork, avocado, mojo sauce, cilantro, and onion. The chef makes fresh guacamole that's a knock-out punch of flavors. Another popular choice is the Uva fries that come topped with chorizo (sausage), spicy crema, cheese curds and, if you simply must, a fried egg, too! If that's not being served when you visit, give the regular sea salt and garlic or sweet potato fries a try. The chopped salad is a great choice. There are plenty of burgers and sandwiches, and those Baja fish tacos are delicious and authentic. All the sandwiches come with garlic fries, but if you're exceptionally hungry, get the Uva fries (when available) for $5 more! Just as at the restaurant upstairs, the choice of beverages is extensive, and the bartenders here know their business.

Earl of Sandwich

ADP: Yes, Cost: $
TYPE: American, Quick Service; Breakfast, Lunch, Dinner

A popular chain, yes, but that doesn't mean the food here is sub-par by any means. This is the first Earl of Sandwich restaurant in California, but the tradition of the hand-held meal dates back to 1762 and the Fourth Earl of Sandwich, John Montagu. The story goes that the lord was enjoying a game of cards and didn't want to take the time to leave his table for a meal. He asked that sliced meat be put between two pieces of bread and the rest is culinary history. The Eleventh Earl of Sandwich is the owner of the eponymous restaurants.

Breakfast sandwiches are served on slightly smaller artisan loaves of bread than those for lunch or dinner. Meats are roasted daily. Expect to find all the usual morning fare like eggs, bacon, ham, cheese, but it's great to see oatmeal, a strawberry yogurt parfait, omelettes, muffins, and fruit as well. The sandwiches at lunch and dinner are a big cut above average. If you're hungry, the Full Montagu ought to satisfy your appetite with generous portions of roast beef, turkey, Swiss, and cheddar. If you'd like to experience the sandwich that started it all, order the Original 1862, roast beef, cheddar, and horseradish. There are a dozen varieties of hot sandwiches, from heavy on the meat to strictly vegetarian.

The Earl has soups, salads, and wraps, too. The berry chicken almond salad is a light, refreshing luncheon option. Get it with a cup of artisan soup made daily, with ingredients according to the season. Another good choice is the Thai wrap with chicken, sweet chili sauce, Chinese veggies, and peanut sauce. Those eating light will surely appreciate the Skinny Earl's quinoa chicken salad or a whole wheat turkey wrap. Cheese or pepperoni pizza breads round out the menu. Salads, pizza, grilled cheese, and turkey and Swiss sandwiches are kids menu items. A usual array of beverages accompany your meal selections, but the dessert menu is much for extensive than you'd imagine. There are more than a dozen kinds of bites, cups, and other sweet temptations.

Jamba Juice

ADP: Yes, Cost: $
TYPE: American, Quick Service; Snack

Jamba Juice is a popular chain with a huge menu. Look for it opposite Naples, within the Grand Californian complex. There are more than two dozen classic fruit smoothies made using healthful ingredients you can feel good about. Pineapple, peach, mango, pomegranate, passion fruit, strawberry, and banana are mixed with yogurt or sherbet for a refreshing snack. More than twenty more are made using simply fruits and juices or veggies. There are two dozen Specialty Smoothies with "boosters" like protein powder, Orange C-Booster, chocolate, and super anti-oxidants. Still hungry?

Check out all the hearty and delicious snack options like cinnamon pretzels, Belgian waffles, Bistro-style sandwiches, oatmeal, and wraps. There are so many types of fresh-squeezed juices that your eyes might cross trying to choose just one! There are many creamy treats, energy bowls, and extras to add like chia or pumpkin seeds, wheatgrass juice, and Greek yogurt. If you can't find what you want here, you just aren't looking hard enough. The menu here is fresh and healthy, but it's also yummy!

La Brea Bakery and Café

ADP: Yes, Cost: $-$$
TYPE: American/Californian, Casual; Brunch, Dinner

Look for La Brea near the entrance to the promenade; it's adjacent to World of Disney and the fountain. It's the brainchild of Nancy Silverman who set the bar pretty high in 1989 at her first bakery. You can watch what's happening in the kitchen or pick up something quick from the new Express, but it you have time (and you might want to book a reservation during busy times and seasons) to settle in and enjoy a leisurely lunch or dinner, give La Brea a try. If the weather's a bit on the nippy side, there are heaters on the outdoor dining patio.

La Brea has several stand-out starters. A particular favorite is the tomato basil bisque or the warm spinach dip, both served in bread bowls. French onion soup is a great choice, too, with La Brea Bakery croutons, melted Gruyère and Parmesan cheese. Sandwiches at brunch are luxuriantly decadent. Blackened mahi mahi, an Angus burger, a short rib grilled cheese, or the veggie burger come sided with pesto pasta salad, fries, or yam chips. Lots of lovely pizzas designed for adults and children join an array of creative, fresh salads. The Montecito salad is a winner with baby spinach and arugula, golden beets, candied walnuts, goat cheese, and a caramelized onion vinaigrette. Get it topped with chicken, shrimp, salmon, or blackened mahi mahi. In the mood for hearty pasta? You'll find plenty to choose from! In addition, the chicken pot pie is a welcome taste of home. Ribs, chicken, salmon, and braised short ribs round out the seasonal specialties.

The kids have a menu with half a dozen options but no Disney check meals. If you chose one of the lighter entrées and can manage dessert, two are exceptional, the dark chocolate ganache cake and the La Brea bread pudding with crème fraiche and caramel sauce. Be aware of the fact that sometimes, the pastries on offer here have been disappointingly less than perfectly fresh, and some guests do complain that the food is not a good value considering the hefty prices. Those looking for a nice glass of wine with their meal may enjoy dining here far more than grabbing something on the run in the theme parks.

La Brea Bakery Express

ADP: Yes, Cost: $
TYPE: American/Californian, Quick Service; Breakfast, Lunch, Dinner

Next to the La Brea Café is this quick express. The menu is decidedly more upscale than many park offerings. Steel cut Irish oatmeal, brioche French toast, a ham or bacon and egg panini, and a croissant breakfast sandwich are all very decent options before the parks open if you arrive early. Lunch sandwiches like ham and Gruyère on a rustic (and occasionally too hard) roll with Dijonaise, grilled chicken, turkey avocado, and more come with mixed greens or chips. Again, bread is the claim to fame at La Brea, but at times, it simply isn't fresh. Individual pizzas and small salads, some with veggies only, are fine if you're in a rush. Gelato, called "black market" due to the dark chocolate, bread pudding, NY cheesecake, and sorbets are the desserts. Kids menu items like grilled cheese, mac and cheese, and chicken tenders are sold at the Express, but no Disney check meals for them. You can get that good tomato basil soup or clam chowder served in a half-pound loaf of county white bread. For people searching out gluten free options, ask because both La Brea Café and Express have them.

Marceline's Confectionary

ADP: Yes, Cost: $
TYPE: American, Quick Service; Snack

Beside Catal and across from Häagen-Dazs is a pretty little shop where you will find a lot to like. As with many of the Disney candy counters, you can watch as employees actually make the treats on sale. Walt Disney spent a happy part of his formative boyhood in Marceline, Missouri, and it's from that small town that the shop takes its name. There are some things that can be made just for you on site like the sour powders so many kids love. If you've never seen how they make those gorgeous and colorful oversized lollipops, this might be your chance. The English toffee is just the right blend of sweet and salty, and those jumbo-sized candy apples are on glorious display—but it's difficult to select just one! They can slice them for you to share. Things at Marcelline's are definitely fresh and there's enough to please most discerning candy lovers. The goodies also make perfect treats to take home as gifts, so pick up some to enjoy right now and some to share with friends and family later.

Naples Ristorante e-Bar

ADP: Yes, Cost: $S
TYPE: Italian, Casual, Table Service; Lunch, Dinner

Naples is at the other end of the little group of restaurants from the Salt and Straw ice cream shop. It has a two-story dining area with lots of ambience and décor inspired by Italy's Carnivale. Reservations are advised, especially during busy times of the day and in busy seasons. Piccoli piotti are small plates to get the party started. The usual Italian appetizers are available like the can't miss La Bruschetta Classica, but so are some new ones like panzerotti, a fried pizza dough filled with mozzarella, ricotta, Parmesan, and marinara.

The minestrone's nice, and there are many ways to order salad from chopped to house to Caesar with add-ons of chicken or shrimp. If you visit in the fall months, you may find the Atunno or autumn salad with kale, roasted pumpkin, Gorgonzola cheese, dried figs, and a balsamic vinaigrette will start your meal off right. Della casa with shrimp includes roasted red peppers, marinated mushrooms, and tomatoes. Many of the standard pasta dishes are available, and the entrées give you plenty of options like salmon, chicken parm, short ribs, and seared fish.

Naples is known for pizza. Find the usual types and a few unusual ones (Gorgonzola, walnut arugula salad, dressed with balsamic vinaigrette) in individual, 20 inch, and half meter sizes. Kids are covered with their own menu and some healthy choices, too.

If you can manage dessert, the tiramisù here is heavenly—smooth, creamy, and a luscious blend of espresso, chocolate, mascarpone, and lady fingers. Lots of people are big fans of the affogato, too, a coffee dessert with espresso poured over vanilla gelato and served with biscotti, and naturally, there's a Siciliani cannoli. Imaginative cocktails (a variety of flights and some Sicilian mules with a big kick), many Italian wines plus some from Spain, France, and Napa, and lots of beers join plenty of non-alcoholic beverages. It is a great option if you're getting a bit weary of the usual park fare and would like to enjoy a full course Italian meal with all the trimmings. You'll definitely pay more, however, for the bump up in quality. A trip to Naples is a great way to expand your dining options and discover some usually good food, attentive service, and an attractive ambience while visiting the Disney resort.

Napolini Pizzeria

ADP: Yes, Cost: $
TYPE: Italian, Quick Service; Breakfast, Lunch, Dinner

Don't have time to sit down and savor? Head for Napolini right next door to Naples. Only during busy seasons, find traditional breakfast choices and croissant sandwiches that are quick and tasty. Get a side of fresh fruit to round out the meal. At lunch and dinner, grab Neapolitan pizza by the slice (California, Roman, Amalfi, Capri, or Vesuvio) with a salad or mac and cheese with a cup of minestrone soup. Turkey pesto, veggie, and prosciutto with salami are some of the sandwich choices. There are half a dozen desserts, and sometimes floats or an Italian ice cream sandwich—brioche filled with gelato—are available. The choices at Napolini are definitely better than those you'll encounter at many of the quick food counters or stands in the theme parks. It's fast, too!

Ralph Brennan's Jazz Kitchen

ADP: Yes, Cost: $$
TYPE: Cajun-Creole, Unique/Themed Dining; Brunch, Lunch, Dinner

A transplant from the Big Easy, Ralph's is situated across from Tortilla Jo's. The place is about as authentic as it gets if you're looking for some genuine N'awlins cookin'. The family hails from New Orleans and bought the Old Absinthe in the French Quarter in 1943. Ralph takes a great deal of personal pride in making sure his guests are happy. Artists from the city were brought in to add special touches to the restaurant's décor. At some 15,000 square feet, the place is enormous. It's two stories tall with an open atrium in the center and wrought iron balustrades that resemble what you'd see in the French Quarter of the old city. The balcony has a panoramic view of Downtown Disney. There is live jazz played nightly. The atmosphere is filled with lively fun, and the food's tasty if a bit pricey. It's busy and popular, so you'd be very wise to book reservations to avoid disappointment.

There are many good reasons why this joint is jumpin'. Brunch—which *may* or may *not* be offered when you visit— is a spirited affair with starters like boudin balls and dirty rice, gumbo ya-ya, the Bourbon Street Sampler, or chicken étouffée soup. Four BIG salads, each a meal, are accompanied by yummy treats like Bananas Foster French Toast or Fruity Pebbles French Toast, the fried green tomato breakfast, crab cakes and eggs, and a Cajun omelette with Andouille sausage. Entrées like red beans and rice, pasta jambalaya, and fried chicken pot pie are unique and full of flavor. The double chocolate bread pudding soufflé requires 25 minutes to prepare, so order it well in advance if you plan to indulge.

Lunch and dinner have similar starters but more of them, and the same goes for BIG salads. Lots of sandwiches, Po' Boys, and burgers are available, and many of the brunch entrées, too. Desserts are what become seriously interesting, however. The beignets here are outstanding. Just follow the trail of powdered sugar outside! They're available to go at the Express. These light, crisp balls of fried dough dusted with powdered sugar are what you saw Tiana serving Big Daddy in *The Princess and the Frog*. Get them with dipping sauce for an extra treat. Bananas Foster is an amazing Southern dessert with rum and brown sugar; if you're celebrating something, it's flambéed tableside for two. The peach cobbler is both traditional and irresistible, and lunch again offers bread pudding and the oh-so-glamourous bananas Foster!

Dinner expands the menu in a way most places don't these days. In addition to all the starters, salads, and sides, there are additional selections of beef, seafood, and poultry. The bacon-wrapped meatloaf's a winner (if it's available), as is the "black and blue" filet mignon with bleu cheese butter and the decadently delicious Southern fried chicken. A large list of beverages featuring a dozen New Orleans specialty drinks (Cat-5 Hurricane, Mint Julep, Creole Pear Mojito), good wines by the glass or bottle, draft beer by the liter or bottled beers should just about cover everyone's preferences. Children are especially well taken care of at Ralph's with many items on a menu made just for them, plenty of fun-sized desserts, and a bevy of non-alcoholic beverages. This jazz-filled restaurant is an experience you won't soon forget, and your choices of dining options either before or after a visit to the theme parks just became a whole lot brighter!

Ralph Brennan's Jazz Kitchen Express

ADP: Yes, Cost: $
TYPE: Cajun-Creole, Quick Service; Lunch, Dinner

Next to the full-service restaurant, find lots of items ready to go quickly at the Express. The breakfast French toast dipper-sticks made from beignets will knock you for a loop! There are regular beignets in sizes of 4, 6, 10 or order 12 bite-sized beignets to go. You'll find big breakfast platters, cereals, breakfast sandwiches, fruit, bacon or sausage, and hash browns.

Lunch and dinner are scaled-down versions of restaurant favorites. Popcorn shrimp, bayou pasta salad with shrimp or chicken, burgers, and sandwiches like the fried chicken with jalapeño-bacon potato salad and Southern cole slaw are good and quick when you just can't spare time to sit down for a leisurely meal. "Little Gators" (children) can request corndog nuggets or popcorn chicken, and there are fountain beverages to go with the order. Whatever you do, don't leave Ralph's without trying the real, New Orleans-style beignets. You simply must see for yourself why they are so ridiculously addictive!

Salt & Straw

ADP: No, Cost: $
TYPE: American, Quick Serve; Snacks

This newer ice cream shop is family-run and features small-batch, seasonal flavors. The owners favor using local ingredients and work closely with farmers in the area. Items rotate frequently, but you can usually count of finding some rustic "slab" pie, cupcakes, and desserts that lean to salted caramel and include unusual additions like pepper or black olive brittle. The flavors are beyond decadent. Chocolate gooey brownie, honey lavender, salted malted chocolate chip cookie dough, roasted strawberry coconut, and seasonally they roll out special flavors. For St. Patrick's Day there was a pots of gold and rainbows flavor which is similar to what you'd find at the wildly popular Milk Bar in NYC.

Splitsville Luxury Lanes—Dining

ADP: Yes, Cost: $$
TYPE: American, Unique/Themed Dining, Table Service; Lunch, Dinner

Splitsville is enormous! 40,000 feet of space with two kitchens and four indoor and outdoor seating locations. It takes you back to the glory days of the 1950s when bowling was the favorite Friday night date spot, but this place is as up-to-date as can be with a two-story tall wall of windows and modern taste favorites like grilled avocado with ahi tuna or scrumptious sushi alongside traditional burgers and fries. If you want to bowl a frame, you'll need to book a lane reservation separate from your dining reservation.

The menu here is longer than both arms put together! Well, that might be a bit of hyperbole, but you get the idea. Apps from fries and chicken tenders to spicy edamame and sliders (vegan or filet) will provide fuel for your fun times. All the classic pizza toppings are on hand as well as some you might not have tried like fig and prosciutto. Almost a dozen sushi specials are available. The crouching dragon with tempura shrimp, avocado, and asparagus is a good choice, but you'll also like the California roll, ninja crunch (crispy tempura salmon), and spicy tuna. The volcano roll is not for the faint of heart with its fiery sriracha and volcano "krab" mix. Handhelds are burgers and sandwiches in a variety of choices from the Foghorn Burger (pepper jack, fried egg, fried jalapeños, and sriracha) to a delicious turkey club supreme and several kinds of chicken.

Entrees and salads, sixteen kinds, include fish and chips, taco bowl, spicy veggies and salmon bowl, poke bowl, steak and mushrooms, and lots more. Kids have many of their favorites available like hot dogs, pizza, chicken tenders, pasta, grilled cheese, and pasta. Large, luscious desserts like "giant" cake (so high, they claim, you'll need a ladder to eat it—talk about a tall tale), Ghirardelli brownie, a super sundae and a root beer float should satisfy any dessert lover.

Many draft and bottled beers, foreign and domestic, along with a big listing of red and white wines should please most discriminating palates. Try something different from the cocktail menu: blue flame, jet juice, rum runner, pink paloma, and more. Not enough? The handcrafted spirits round out the long drinks menu with vintage favorites such as the Moscow Mule and modern trend setters like royal sangria, Cali crush, and watermelon smash. Bring the kids, bring your friends, bring Mom and Pop, and leave room for some of the most fun assortment of food and beverages in all of Downtown Disney—and don't forget to bowl while you're here!

Sprinkles
ADP: Yes, Cost: $
TYPE: American, Quick Service; Snack

This is it, the one and only genuine original, the cupcake place that launched America's cupcake obsession. In addition to the dessert that made Sprinkles a legend, you'll find lots of cookies (chocolate chip, fudge brownie, peanut butter pretzel chip, snickerdoodle, salted caramel oatmeal, and more) and drinks (milk, water, apple juice, soda) as well. The famous flavors usually on hand include: black and white, dark chocolate, vanilla, cinnamon sugar, chocolate marshmallow, red velvet, vanilla with chocolate, triple cinnamon, in addition to other seasonal daily selections. You won't be disappointed at Sprinkles.

Starbucks and Starbucks West

ADP: No, Cost: $
TYPE: American, Quick Service; Snacks

With medium roast, dark roast, espresso drinks, Clover-brand brewed coffee when available, teas, hot chocolate, lemonade, apple juice, bottled drinks, and smoothies, you'll find something that will go exactly right with your choice of either something from the bakery or a hot breakfast sandwich. Starbucks also carries oatmeal, bistro boxes, more than a dozen kinds of cold sandwiches, yogurt, fruit, and seasonal treats. There's something for almost anyone at Starbucks, and the quality is good. They open early and close late, so stopping by either one of the two, one opposite World of Disney and the other opposite LEGO, will fit practically all schedules, too

Taqueria at Tortilla Jo's

ADP: Yes, Cost: $
TYPE: Mexican, Quick Service; Breakfast, Lunch, Dinner

Taqueria means taco shop, and you'll find tacos and more at this one. You can get them made to order just the way you want. For breakfast, there are half a dozen kinds of breakfast burritos in addition to Mexican favorites like chiliquiles, huevos rancheros, a breakfast "bowl" in a tortilla shell, and Mexican oatmeal or a fruit and yogurt bowl.

Lunch and dinner give you a chance to choose your entire entrée (taco, burrito, bowl, or nachos), your protein (steak, chicken, beef, pork, or veggie), your fillings (beans, cheese, rice, lettuce, onions and cilantro, or pico de gallo), and you can choose to add a side and a drink. There are items designed especially for kids and fountain drinks. If you want a simple dessert, they have those, too including some real Mexican candy and palettes (ice pops) as well as brownies, cookies, and fruit. The ability to customize is helpful, especially if you have group members with distinct preferences.

Tortilla Jo's

ADP: Yes, Cost: $S
TYPE: Mexican, Casual,Themed Dining, Table Service; Brunch, Lunch, Dinner

Both the Taqueria and Tortilla Jo's are right across the walkway from Ralph Brennan's Jazz Kitchen. At Jo's, you'll find many areas to dine from cozy and intimate rooms to a wide-open plaza strung with lights. If you have a preference be sure to specify, and it's a good idea to make reservations in advance. The casual, sit-down service allows you to relax in a pretty Mexican setting, and the breakfast menu has something for every taste from Americano to strictly Mexicano. French toast and eggs American style with bacon or sausage are fine, but there are spicy entrées like breakfast burritos and enchiladas, eggs and Mexican sausage, chiliquiles, and huevos rancheros, too. Some come with dessert mini-chimis stuffed with apples. There are plenty of beers, cocktails, and non-alcoholic drinks. The kids can get buttermilk pancakes or a scrambled egg platter.

At lunch and dinner, there is a nice variety of starters to keep you happy. Jo's does a fun tableside guacamole, and the empanadas are delicious. There are also many sorts of nachos (try the signature barbacoa, which means barbecued beef) and ceviche if you're a fan of the raw seafood dish from Latin America. There are half a dozen nice salads and street tacos in favorite flavors—asada (steak), pollo (chicken), pescado (fish), and carnitas (pork). If you've never had these, you're in for a treat! They're sided with Mexican red rice and beans. There are burritos served seven ways, several kinds of enchiladas, and house specialties featuring pork, chicken, beef, and seafood. If you're famished, consider one of the combination plates where you can choose two of three of the items and have Mexican rice or sautéed veggies on the side.

Speaking of sides, you can always add some to any order from sweet corn cakes to nopales rancheros—sautéed cactus leaves. Don't worry, these have no needles. Jo's has twenty kinds of Margaritas, and some folks come especially for the drinks here. Mojitos are popular, along with a long listing of beers, and wines from Spain, France, and California are available by the bottle or glass. If you have time for a trip south of the border,

Jo's menu is a welcome change from the usual park foods, but don't think of it as a "quick" stop. Unfortunately, sometimes the service has been very slow and sporadic, and some servers either haven't been properly trained or perhaps need some retraining. The tableside guac is great, but if your food is late and improperly cooked, that can spoil the entire experience. Don't suffer in silence. Ask a manager for assistance, should this happen to you. Also note that there are strolling female mariachi band members and a person makes ballon animals sometimes, which you may or may not appreciate.

Wetzel's Pretzels

ADP: Yes, Cost: $
TYPE: American, Quick Service; Snack

Look for the pretzel counter across from Catal, and you'll soon agree that Wetzel's doesn't disappoint! You might have thought you knew pretzels, but wait just a minute! What about almond crunch, sinful cinnamon, pepperoni twist, sour cream and onion, jalapeño cheese, or the new Jalaroni? Don't overlook the plain ones, either. Warm, salty, soft and bigger than two fists, these don't come shaped like your old pal, Mickey, but they're still a big leap forward from your average pretzel. Get them in "bits" meaning bite-sized and with dips like cheese, caramel, or pizza sauce. You'll be thirsty, so get a lemonade, or better yet a frozen lemonade, in regular or strawberry flavor along with it. Granitas and frozen fountain drinks are available as well. If it isn't time for lunch or dinner but you're hungry, this portable feast may be exactly what you need. It's hard to imagine that the humble pretzel could be this tasty!

CHAPTER SEVEN

Disneyland Resort Hotels: Grand Californian Hotel & Spa, Disneyland Hotel, Paradise Pier Hotel

Disney's Grand Californian

If you appreciate the style of the Arts and Crafts movement, you'll love this beautiful hotel. It's the most luxurious (and most expensive) of the resort accommodations. The goal was "to bring the outdoors in," and the lush plantings of the landscape surround it in leafy splendor. It was built in 2001, along with a big expansion of the park, and a new Disney Vacation Club wing was added on in 2009. In 2017, the entire hotel underwent a refurbishment. There are more than a thousand rooms, suites, and villas, and about three hundred underground parking spaces. If you've ever visited Wilderness Lodge at Walt Disney World, you'll note many similarities. They were both designed by Peter Dominik and call to mind some of those grand old hotels in the National Parks like the Old Faithful Inn at Yellowstone or California's Majestic Yosemite Hotel (formerly the Ahwanee). There's even a direct access to Disney's California Adventure near the area known as Grizzly Peak. All those guests need places to eat, of course, and there are several excellent choices. You needn't stay here to enjoy dining here.

Hearthstone Lounge

ADP: No, Cost: $-$$
TYPE: American/Californian, Bars and Lounges, Table Service; Snacks, Lunch, Dinner

The lounge itself is beautiful, a tribute to the original national park hotels. Sit by the fire if you want to get cozy and order from a very nice variety of foods and drinks. Two special Mickey goodies are available seasonally, the Mickey-shaped artisanal pizza and the oh-so-impressive Mickey's baked Alaska—chocolate ice cream robed in brûléed meringue with raspberry sauce. Tasty apps vary seasonally. Some recent ones are the succulent wagyu burgers, avocado toast, fish tacos, charcuterie with fromaga (cheese), and a good old-fashioned jumbo shrimp cocktail that's been updated with Yuzu (twisted Japanese lemon) cocktail sauce. Four crowd-pleasing pizzas go well with the tremendously extensive list of cool cocktails just like the ones you'll find at Napa Rose. There are also red and white sangrias and beers to suit just about any aficionado. Just as at Napa Rose, you'll find a seriously expansive wine list at your fingertips including some sparkling wines. This lounge is a great spot to hang out between time spent in the parks, to refresh, and to recuperate while satisfying any hunger pangs you might be experiencing. The mood is casually upscale.

Napa Rose

ADP: No, Cost: $$$$
TYPE: American/Californian, Fine/Signature Dining, Table Service; Dinner

This particular restaurant isn't simply outstanding when compared with other theme park restaurants, Napa Rose a stand-out place for a luxury meal all on its own. The Zagat guide gives it a rating of 4.5/5. Reservations are a must, and you should be aware that hotel guests do get priority when booking at any of the Disneyland resort restaurants. There-fore, you're going to need to be flexible and arrange for your table *well* in advance of your arrival. Great food, service, and ambience won't come cheap, and meals at the Rose will run $60 and more—sometimes quite a bit more! If you're expect-ing huge portions, look elsewhere. This is not one of those places that has a menu longer than your arm, but everything on the menu is absolutely choice. In addition, you may contact Chef Andrew Sutton for a personal (and pricey) menu experience, sit at the Chef's Counter, or choose the *prix fixe* Vintner's Table, about $100.

For starters, the sautéed Diver scallop is a good choice, as is the famous smiling tiger salad that features Asian greens, spicy beef, lobster shrimp fritters, with a delicious coconut vinaigrette. Last season there were choices some of us found a mite too adventurous like the lamb or hamachi tartare (raw); the gnochette with lobster, mushrooms, and veal sweetbreads (an animal's thymus gland or pancreas) falls into the same category, but true gourmands may well desire to sample out-of-the-ordinary offerings such as those. The scallops and smiling tiger are fixtures, but rabbit bratwurst, goose ragu (ragout) and roasted oysters have been added. The roasted apple and thyme salad with French cheddar and walnuts is simple and delightful.

One thing you must understand is that menu at this upscale venue changes frequently, more so than it does at most places. This sometimes leads to disappointment if what you anticipated is missing, but it's a fact of life at outstanding restaurants. You may find some cuts of wild boar or wild boar meatloaf, a small pizza, octopus, or duck meatballs for starters, so be aware that these are *recent* starters and will provide an idea of the kind of things you may expect, although specific items may very well not be available when you visit. The same is true with soups and salads, sometimes warm salads, which are fresh and based on seasonal ingredients. For entrées, you'll usually find a fresh fish of the day and a fresh sustainable fish, a free-range chicken dish, a really wonderful and well-prepared cut of steak or two, lamb, and sometimes bison or occasionally duck. The entrées are accompanied by a la carte sides like roasted fingerling potatoes, truffled mac and cheese orecchiette pasta, or braised greens. Children have plenty on their menu to please most young diners. They'll choose from pasta, cheese pizza, fish, beef, and chicken entrees.

The desserts are legendary at Napa Rose, so try to save some room. The Valrhona Chocolate and Salted Caramel

Crèmeux is not only visually gorgeous, it tastes amazing! The pretzel-streusel topping includes brown sugar, and it comes with dark chocolate-stout ice cream, the perfect complement. You might find a cornmeal citrus upside down cake, tres leches cake, or white chocolate crumble tart with strawberries worthy of ending your perfect meal. Really feeling indulgent? Then opt for the chocolate truffle hazelnut crunch cake bar with a bananas foster compote. There are many kinds of house-made ice creams and sorbets in exotic flavors, while kids have their own choices of desserts from brownies to the creative Balboa Beach Sand, a pretty little crème brûlée sea with graham cracker sand, topped with a tiny umbrella and some edible gummy fish—such fun for kids.

The cocktails and beers are definitely worth a second (or even a third) look. You'll find all the traditionally popular cocktails, along with house favorites like the Napa Rose, the Rennie Rose, and the Napa Passion. Almost two dozen beers from pale to stout are available, not to mention a wine list that compares well to the very best available. There are a good many California wines, naturally, but you'll see reds from Tuscany, France, South Africa, and more. The white are just as impressive, and regardless of what you had in mind, the helpful sommelier can recommend just the perfect one to complement your choice of entrée. The wine list boasts more than sixty excellent vintages.

Visit Napa Rose if you have a special celebration or just because you want a truly first class dining experience. Be extremely clear about expectations, reserve your table well in advance, and then sit back and enjoy the entire experience. If you can't find an opening, you can always try the Napa Lounge where many of the menu items and all of the drinks served in the restaurant are also available.

Note: Starting March 30, 2019, "A Fairytale Experience for Everyone" began at Napa Rose

If you've never had the pleasure of dining with the Disney Princesses, this is sure to be a highlight of your Disney visit! You'll have a scrumptious three-course breakfast to enjoy while a rotating cast of the royal young ladies stop by your table for a chat, to pose for picture, and to sign autographs. A portrait with your personal Princess will be taken and you'll also receive a keepsake. These experiences are why you come to the parks, so indulge yourself and your family. Just realize that special dining like this won't come cheap—you'll pay top dollar, but in this case, it honestly is worth every penny, especially if you have a little Prince or Princess of your own.

Napa Rose Lounge

ADP: No, Cost: $$/$$$
TYPE: American/Californian, Fine/Signature Dining; Dinner

This luxurious lounge is a stunning spot to sample some of the great appetizers and drinks or maybe a late-night dessert with a nightcap at the end of a busy day. See the Napa Rose review for an idea of some of the kinds of choices you'll find. All the wines, beers, cocktails, and specialty drinks are available. The setting is gorgeous, and the service is great. It's a top pick! If you aren't able to secure a reservation at the Napa Rose, try the lounge.

Storyteller's Café

ADP: Yes, Cost: $$$
TYPE: American, Family Style/Buffet, Character Dining (breakfast and brunch only), Unique/Themed Dining, Table Service; Breakfast, Lunch, Weekend Brunch, Dinner

The food is extremely good here, but many people come for the characters. They only appear at breakfast and brunch. Some special holiday brunches are prepared. No particular characters are guaranteed, but those who visit come to meet and greet guests at every table. It's a convenient way to snap photos, get autographs, and save long waits in line to meet characters in the theme parks.

Lunch and dinner are served à la carte; *no* characters visit during those meals. Reservations are highly recommended. Tables can be hard to get during busy seasons at the parks, so reserve yours well in advance. Zagat rates it 4.2, and be aware that prices are steep. Breakfast has all the American favorites you'd expect like eggs Benedict, omelettes cooked to order, sometimes a special caramel French toast, Mickey waffles, lots of breakfast pastries, bagels and lox, and plenty of fresh, seasonal fruit. Alcoholic beverages are available and sold separately. You'll find mimosas, bloody Marys, and champagne, along with Joffrey's coffee, tea, milk, and juices.

Brunch expands the menu considerably. Salads, potatoes, chiliquiles, chicken, pork, veggies, and a full range of hot or cold cereals are offered in addition to all the regular breakfast buffet items; there are some delicious dessert options if you're in the mood. Try the warm bread pudding with vanilla sauce.

Lunch, added during busy seasons, has a large variety of soups and salads, but the place is justifiably famous for the addictive Nebraska roasted corn chowder—and it's delicious! There are four artisanal pizzas. For two with pizazz, try the lemon-shrimp or the 'Nduja Prosciutto Sausage Pizza. Classic wedge or Caesar salads can be ordered with salmon or chicken or shrimp. Other entrees include the melt-in-your mouth Wagyu burger, a decadent Croque Monsieur, steak frites, and a very nice short-rib grilled cheese sided with fries, chips, or fruit. Chocolate fans can indulge in the popular chocolate chip cookie skillet or the molten chocolate cake. Cheesecake, bread pudding, and crème brûlée and other seasonal desserts are featured if you can manage after your lunch.

Dinner is even more extensive than lunch (don't skip that charred—or roasted— corn chowder) with a tremendous variety of beef, chicken, and seafood entrées added in addition to many of the lunch items. There are cocktails, wines, and beers to suit just about any taste, in addition to many non-alcoholic specialty beverages, fountain drinks, and coffee, tea, and milk. Kids, always very welcome at Storyteller's, will find Disney Check meal choices and lots of their own favorite desserts here. The setting is lovely, the food beautifully prepared, and the character meals are delightful. No matter which meal you choose, a visit to Storyteller's Café is always a genuine treat!

White Water Snacks

ADP: Yes, Cost: $$/$$$
TYPE: American, Quick Service, Mobile Orders; Breakfast, Lunch, Dinner

Designed to mimic a campground, camping was never quite like this! For an on-the-go meal, count on fast service and better-than-serviceable food. Breakfast sometimes has some fun choices like mini-cinnamon rolls and Mickey waffles. There are breakfast sandwiches and burritos, as well as chiliquiles. Tater tots come loaded or as part of the American breakfast. There is a roasted veggie quiche, a three-cheese quiche, and a Belgian waffle. Many beverages on the menu ought to quench your thirst.

At lunch, find burgers, rice bowls with beef or chicken, grilled cheese with fries or fruit, and spectacular nachos loaded with just about anything you can imagine. Skewers include the shawarma chicken, Mediterranean vegetable, or bulgogi beef. Those special Grand Californian pizzas can be ordered right here. The margherita or charcuterie are great choices! Kids can get a Disney check turkey sandwich or from the regular kids menu they'll find nuggets, burgers, and grilled cheese. Dinner menu is identical to lunch. There are some good cupcakes seasonally, or a root beer float and a seasonal crostada (rustic Italian baked tart) with Chantilly cream. Don't overlook this place.

Disneyland Hotel

Way back when Disneyland was just an idea and Anaheim felt like it was located smack dab in the middle of nowhere, Walt quickly realized that people who visited his theme park would want a place to stay. His finances were already stretched to the limit, however, so the Disneyland Hotel was built, owned, and operated by Jack Wrather and Maria Helen Alvarez. It opened to the public on October 5, 1955 with about one hundred rooms spread out among five two-story wings. Rooms went for $15 a night, about $140 today. Five years later, the number of rooms had tripled. Trams transported the first guests to the park, but in 1961, the Monorail opened a new station at the hotel. By the time Walt could well afford to buy the hotel, Wrather wouldn't sell. It was a prestigious, lucrative property that just kept getting bigger and better. A few months after Wrather died, Michael Eisner took over the Disney company. Following the 1988 death of Wrather's widow, Hollywood actress Bonita Granville, the Disney organization finally secured ownership of the Disneyland Hotel—but they had to buy Wrather's entire company to get it! The old buildings were surrounded by gardens and lush, tropical vegetation. There was a miniature golf course on the property right next to the old Ball Road that was made to resemble a tiny Disneyland. Helicopters landed regularly transporting guests to and fro between LAX and the hotel. Now, sadly, none of the original hotel buildings remain. Like much of the mid-century California architecture, it didn't survive modernization.

Goofy's Kitchen

ADP: Yes, Cost: $$$
TYPE: American, Buffet/Family Style, Character Dining; Breakfast, Dinner

It can be difficult to connect with costumed characters in the parks, but at a character buffet, they come right to your table, pose for pictures, sign autographs, and interact with your party. No waiting in lines! Few do a buffet like Disney, and even the pickiest eater can find plenty to choose from.

At breakfast, there are omelette stations, Mickey pancakes and waffles, breakfast meats, pastries, fresh fruit, chicken nuggets, Goofy's peanut butter pizza, French toast, and eggs Benedict. Lots of crafty cocktails and specialty tea and coffee drinks go well with the menu items. If you haven't done a character buffet, come see what you've been missing. The adults enjoy them every bit as much as the younger visitors.

For dinner, there's a carving station, fresh fish, grilled hot dogs, pizza, fresh fruit, veggies, salads, mac and cheese, and for dessert there is a station stocked with sweets and a soft-serve yogurt bar with toppings. Goofy will greet you, but the selection of other characters rotates, so be prepared to be surprised.

Steakhouse 55

ADP: Yes, Cost: $$$
TYPE: American, Fine/Signature Dining, Table Service; Breakfast, Afternoon Tea, Dinner

It's hard to beat the comfort and consistency of a traditional Steakhouse, and here you'll be treated to all the familiar hallmarks of a good one from the rich wood paneling to the luxuriously elegant seating to vintage photos of Walt Disney and other Hollywood luminaries from the past gracing the walls. Why 55? That's a nod to the year Disneyland opened. You can book the Oak Room for private gatherings of up to 24 guests.

Should you decide to linger over breakfast, this is the perfect spot to do it. Good old steak and eggs fit the bill nicely, and there are hearty choices like chicken and waffles, eggs Benedict, French toast, or omelettes, but health-conscious offerings like the lighter continental breakfast or steel-cut oatmeal with fruit are also available. A Disney check meal for the kids and several other kid-friendly favorites (Mickey pancakes, cinnamon French toast, cereals) or any number of appetizing a la carte items will send you on your way ready for a big day at one of the parks.

Afternoon tea is a decadent indulgence for those guests ready to take a pampered break in their day. It's available from noon to 3:00 p.m. on Friday, Saturday and Sunday. Select from the Classic, the Premium, or Kids Tea Parties. Scones, tea sandwiches, deserts, loose-leaf tea, and other delectable standards are served. Occasionally, you'll find Mickey-and-Minnie-themed tea parties, and the treats then are every bit as visually stunning as they are delicious.

The main event here, however, is the steak dinner just like it was presented back in the middle of the last century. Crab cakes are a good choice for your appetizer, and the velvety Maine lobster bisque or rustic onion soup au gratin are equally impressive. Salads run from the familiar "wedge" to the more trendy baby kale and beets with candied pepitas (pumpkin seeds) and orange segments. Steaks are the stars, and that 18-ounce bone-in rib eye is glorious at a pricey $59. The filet, prime rib, and NY strip loin are guaranteed to satisfy hearty appetites. If you aren't in the mood for a steak, take a look at the Maine lobster tail, salmon, a bone-in Tomahawk pork chop, chicken, or lamb.

Children may select from chicken pot pie, a filet, shrimp scampi, and orange-glazed salmon. After a big dinner with all the trimmings, it might be difficult to even *think* about dessert, but wait a minute. Steakhouse 55 has a famous 24-layer chocolate cake that will knock your socks off! Mint chocolate chip gelato, Nutella, milk and dark chocolate, sandwiched between chocolate sponge layers make for an impressive *fin* to a memorable dinner. Ask the sommelier for assistance in selecting just the right wine to accompany your menu choice. A meal here is sure to be an indulgent splurge in every way. If you can't get a reservation, and they're *highly* advised, try the Steakhouse 55 Lounge. You'll find many of the same options.

Tangaroa Terrace Tropical Bar & Grill

ADP: Yes, Cost: $
TYPE: American, Fast/Casual Dining, Mobile Orders; Breakfast, Lunch, Dinner

If the name rings a bell, that's because you've probably met Tangaroa, god of the sea, in the Enchanted Tiki Room, Disneyland's first audio-animatronic attraction. The swaying palms and tropical tiki torches will call to mind the South Sea islands, as will the cuisine. Dine inside or al fresco.

Breakfast offers a generous platter of scrambled eggs, bacon, hash browns, and island fruit. The Tangaroa Toast is scrumptios and a hugely popular favorite. It's "brick" toast (think big!) with bananas Foster, whipped cream, toasted coconut, and island fruit. Pineapple upside down pancakes are another crowd pleaser, a nod to one of Walt's favorite desserts. There's a Kahlua-style pulled pork sandwich with hash browns and a fried egg, as well as an Açaí Chia Breakfast Bowl with granola.

Kids can opt for Disney Check meals with their own breakfast platter or the Power Pack. They'll also find Mickey-shaped Tangaroa toast and those delicious pineapple upside down pancakes on their menu. Take along fruit, pastries, and beverages from the Grab 'n' Go section. The coffee listings are extensive and you can also get the famous Dole Whip right here without the sometimes-long lines in Adventureland. Note that if you have dietary restrictions or allergies in your party, gluten/wheat-free, peanut/tree nut-free, soy-free, fish/shellfish free, and egg-free choices abound at Tangaroa.

Lunch and dinner are casual and fun. Angus cheeseburgers, Kalua poutine, lentil garden bowl, chili garlic edamame, nachos, salads, the traditional pu pu platter (small meat and seafood apps), pork goyoza, Hawaiian platter, and sweet and spicy chicken wings will add to the island atmosphere when dining here. Disney check meals include a grilled salmon bowl and the power pack meal. Kids have a cheeseburger or chicken nuggets, also. As with breakfast, the Grab 'n' Go section is a definite perk to dining here, since you can take fruit, baked goods, beverages, and Dole Whip right along with you as you head out to explore the parks.

The Coffee House

ADP: Yes, Cost: $
TYPE: American, Quick Service; Snack

For something light and easy when you're short on time, you can get a quick sandwich, salad, or fruit plate at this convenient little place. Healthful snacks like yogurt, fresh fruit, cereal, and a protein bar are options, as is a nice assortment of delicious, decadent pastries. Bagels, muffins, gourmet donuts, cinnamon rolls, croissants, and those gorgeous seasonal cupcakes go nicely with the wide choice of espresso specialities, coffees, and drinks like tea and hot chocolate. Milk and juices along with water and lemonade are sold, too, at the well-stocked Coffee House.

Trader Sam's Enchanted Tiki Bar

ADP: Yes, Cost: $, $$
TYPE: American, Bars and Lounges, Table Service; Lounge

Who doesn't love Trader Sam, intrepid collector of shrunken heads who'll gladly trade two of his for one of yours? He serves up Hawaiian cheeseburgers, shipwreck nachos, pork gyoza, the ever-popular pu pu platter, a kid's power-pack Disney check meal, and enough specialty drinks to make your head spin—literally. There are no-booze brews, draft and bottled beers, sparkling wines, reds and whites, plus two sangrias. The tropical island décor at Sam's is spot on.

Disney's Paradise Pier Hotel

The hotel opened in 1984 as Emerald of Anaheim and then the name changed to the Pan-Pacific. It was designed as a fifteen story tower with about two dozen suites. Bought by the Disney Company in 1995, the name was changed again to Disneyland Pacific. In 2000, it was rebranded yet again. Since the hotel overlooks the Paradise Pier area in Disney's California Adventure, it took that name for the view from many of the rooms. With 481 rooms and 25 suites, it has a beach theme that gives a nod to the grand oceanside pavilions of the 1920s. On the hotel's roof, there's a pool with a wild, twisty waterslide called California Streamin' inspired by the park's old California Screamin' roller coaster, a pool just for the kids, and the adult Paradise spa whirlpool. At night, the pool area affords the perfect view of Disneyland fireworks. This is the most budget-friendly of the three resort hotels.

Disney's PCH Grill

ADP: Yes, Cost: $$/$$$
TYPE: American, Buffet/Family Style, Casual Dining, Character Dining (at breakfast and brunch only); Breakfast, Brunch (only on Fridays, Saturdays, and Sundays), Dinner

Anyone familiar with California knows PCH is the acronym for Pacific Coast Highway, that glorious stretch of road that hugs the rocky coastline as it passes by some of the most beautiful, breathtaking scenery in the state.

Characters like Donald Duck and his best buddies will join you at breakfast spending time at every table. New Seaside Brunches are scheduled for Friday, Saturday, and Sunday beginning March 29, 2019. The meal starts with fruit, pastries, an oatmeal station, a smoked salmon station, and a parfait bar where you create your own. Eggs, breakfast meats, an egg-white frittata, breakfast flatbreads, chiliquiles, and grilled chicken are the entrées. Kids have Mickey waffles, Minnie pancakes, or chocolate-banana stuffed French toast.

Dinner has no characters. It is meant to suggest a beach-side bonfire buffet. There are plenty of choices that should keep everyone full. There are turkey and roast beef carving stations, stations featuring chicken Alfredo, pizza, mini hot dogs, salmon, ribs, pizza, shrimp and mussel cioppino, and many sides to round of your dinner from potatoes, mac and cheese, and rice pilaf to all sorts of veggies and chicken noodle soup. Want to custom build your own nachos? Go ahead! How about a make your own salad station? If you don't want to make your own, your find plenty of kinds to choose from like cold potato, cous cous, fruit, and Caesar.

Desserts? Of course! Look for mini-cheesecakes in seasonal flavors, strawberry shortcake, brownies, lemon bars, and that ol' bonfire classic—S'mores you put together yourself. If your party likes meals made to individual specifications, the chance to create your own plate taking exactly what you want and leaving the rest, PCH might just be the perfect spot for your next meal.

Surfside Lounge

ADP: Yes, Cost: $$/$$$
TYPE: American, Bars and Lounges; Breakfast, Lunch, Dinner

If you're staying at the Pier, a stop at the Surfside Lounge is a convenient way to have a quick, filling meal before heading off on a Disney adventure.

Breakfast includes all the standard American favorites with a few more unusual options tossed in for good measure. French toast and pancakes, eggs Benedict, omelets, a croissant breakfast sandwich, and the big American breakfast are available, as is a smoked salmon platter with toasted bagel or the breakfast burrito with queso fresco, shredded beef, and scrambled eggs. Lighter fare includes fresh fruit, oatmeal, yogurt parfait, or a tropical smoothie. Kids can load up on Mickey pancakes and waffles or the junior scramble. No Disney check meals, however. Juices, milk, espresso blends, hot chocolate, and coffee done just about any way you like it should get you through the morning.

Lunch and dinner offer you many choices, too. Nothing here will match some of the finest dining opportunities at the resort, but you'll certainly have no trouble finding something filling and tasty without busting the budget. Apps like ahi tuna, wings, nachos with chicken or beef, guac and tortilla chips, pork sliders, and a yummy house-made pozole (pronounced po-ZO-lay, it means hominy and is a Mexican-style stew made from beans and meat topped with fresh garnishes), will get your meal started. The usual wedge and Caesar salads are joined by an arugula and fennel salad with roasted beets, oranges, and a goat cheese spread, and the kale and quinoa salad with chia dressing. Typical pizzas in four styles and entrees from a build-your-own poke bowl to cheeseburgers, salmon burgers, a turkey club, and mini street tacos al pastor (pork) are crowd-pleasers. The items lean toward a Mexican influence, but it's definitely *American* Mexican and not too spicy for most people.

If you've never treated the family to one of Disney's famous Kitchen Sink Sundaes, here's your opportunity! It's just what it sounds like—everything you could wish for in a sundae is tossed together in a souvenir kitchen sink. Sundaes, shakes, and cake are choices if you can't quite polish of a "Sink." Kids have one Disney check meal, grilled chicken breast with fresh fruit and veggies, or they can choose a kids meal hamburger or chicken nuggets.

In addition to all those breakfast beverages, you'll find a huge variety of clever cocktails (Walk the Plank, Magical Star Cocktail, Antioxidant Lemonade, Smoked Turkey—with Wild Turkey 101 Bourbon, and *lots* more). Red wines, white wines, and more than two dozen varieties of beer plus a few "mocktails" will wet your whistle as you dine. The Surfside Lounge isn't an especially memorable dining experience, but it will certainly fill you up at "Disney-reasonable" prices, it's convenient if you're staying at the Pier, and there is plenty to choose from on the big menu.

The Sand Bar

ADP: Yes, Cost: $/$$
TYPE: American, Quick Serve; Snacks, Lunch, Dinner

Only open seasonally, this walk-up counter is located on the pool deck of the Paradise Pier Hotel. Some people who stay here regularly don't realize it's even here, and it isn't open year-round. Check during your stay for hours and availability. A full-service bar menu caters to adult specialty beverage needs. They usually have foot-long all-beef hot dogs, cheeseburgers, a chicken pita or turkey sandwich, chef salads, and chicken quesadillas. If you just want a drink and a side, there are nachos, the Mickey pretzel, whole fruit, fries, and house-made chips. Kids will even find a Disney check meal turkey sandwich with grapes and carrot sticks. Other kids meal alternatives are a beef hot dog, hamburger, mixed fruit cup, and frozen treats. The bar stocks lemonade, smoothies, water, and milk. On a hot day, the convenient Sand Bar is just what you want!

CHAPTER EIGHT

Disney California Adventure: Buena Vista Street and Hollywood Land

Disney California Adventure

When first imagined in 1991, it was to be called WestCOT, the western counterpart to Disney World's EPCOT, whose name later changed to Epcot. Names, just like attractions, come and go frequently at the Disney theme parks. The price tag for such an expensive undertaking, though, was too much for the company to bear. Euro Disneyland, renamed Disneyland Paris, wasn't an immediate success. Money was tight.

By 1995, Michael Eisner and top Disney execs put their heads together at a meeting in Aspen and instead came up with building a theme park homage to California. The inspiration was to take some of the state's best-known, beloved tourist attractions and create a place where the spirit and history of the Golden State would be celebrated. Ground was broken on January 22, 1998, in what had been for the past forty years Disneyland's expansive parking lot. By opening day, February 8, 2001, hopes were running high for tremendous crowds and immediate financial success. Instead, the original four districts with their twenty-two shows and attractions and fifteen restaurants received a quiet, utterly unimpressed "ho-hum" from guests. There might as well have been tumbleweeds blowing past the big Ferris wheel.

There was no berm, that high barrier of earth and grass, that keeps the rest of the world out and allows Disneyland to feel cozily isolated from reality. Things were too generic, too corny. In some ways, it felt closer to a parody than an homage. The focus was on adults, while children seemed to have been largely forgotten. There was an overabundance of shops and places to eat and not nearly enough entertainment. In short, Disney's California Adventure (as it was first called), was a disappointment to company management and visitors alike. Underwhelmed was the consensus opinion of visitors. Word of mouth, instead of stoking excitement and demand as anticipated, was sounding a premature death knell before the place had a chance to find an identity.

By the time Bob Iger had taken over the company reins, it was high time to make some major changes in an enterprise that was more of a flop than a hit. In October of 2007, a much-needed $1.1 billion expansion, near-total redesign of the park, and the addition of two additional lands was announced. By June 15, 2012, the park was a lot closer to what you'll experience today, and that's when it became known as Disney California Adventure, losing the cumbersome possessive apostrophe s. For years, Disneyland at 85 acres had remained reliably busy while DCA at 72 acres was vastly underutilized.

Today, attendance is pretty evenly split between the two theme parks. The newest addition to the park scheduled to open in 2020 will be called Marvel Land and will feature attractions inspired by Marvel Comics Guardians of the Galaxy, Spider-Man, and the Avengers. From a seriously shaky, altogether uninspired beginning, the second of the Anaheim theme parks has finally found its footing and is up and running as Disneyland's shiny, successful younger sibling.

Buena Vista Street

The pretty Spanish description means "good view," and as far as Disney's concerned, the view from Buena Vista has been very good indeed. The Disney studios in Burbank, California, are located on Buena Vista Street. Back in 1953, *Peter Pan* was the first Disney motion picture to be released by the Buena Vista Distribution company. Before 27,000 acres of undeveloped land in Orlando, Florida, had caught Walt's eye, Black

Lake was just a small body of water in the back country of the sunshine state. Now, it's the location of the famous Walt Disney World Resort; the lake was swiftly rechristened Lake Buena Vista. The city Disney built there also adopted the name. Therefore, it made perfect sense to call the street leading into Disney California Adventure Lake Buena Vista Street, changed from its original name, Sunshine Plaza. The area harkens back to the 1920s when the Disney brothers, Walt and Roy, arrived from Missouri to find fame and fortune. It will remind you of Main Street, U.S.A., in Disneyland. It's a gateway to the central hub that fans out to other areas of the park. It has trolley rides like Disneyland, but whereas Main Street set in about 1900-1910 has horse-drawn trolleys, Buena Vista Street reminiscent of 1920-1930 has the Red Car Trolley based on the vintage Pacific Electric's old Red Car line. There's no castle. Instead, the Carthay Circle Theatre replica where *Snow White and the Seven Dwarfs* premiered in 1937 and *Fantasia* in 1941 anchors the far end of a street that's lined with attractive shops and places to grab a quick snack or sit down and savor a meal.

Kiosks, Wagons, and Carts

- Look for a couple of well-supplied **Ice Cream Carts** at the end of the street to the right off the central hub as you ride the trolley from the entrance. Big, fluffy clouds of pink or blue cotton candy are sold on paper cones, along with a selection of frozen novelties. Nearly everyone loves the iconic Premium Mickey ice cream bars and Mickey ice cream sandwiches. The carts stock frozen bananas covered in chocolate, an old California beach treat—try one if you haven't already because they are amazing. Coke products, frozen fruit bars, frozen lemonade, and water may also be found at the carts.

- Your nose will surely lead you here, but just in case, find a silver Deco-style **Popcorn Cart** on the left side of the street on the way into Hollywood Land. Popcorn has become an industry all its own at Disney. Gone are the rectangular little blue and white boxes that could be had for one thin dime at Disneyland in 1955. A regular scoop is now $5.00, but it's hot and fresh and many guests find it addictive. Souvenir collectible buckets are all the rage. Get one for $9, or get a premium bucket for $16. Caramel popcorn is sold here, as are Coke products and water. In Tokyo where popcorn is king, you'll find flavors like curry (the current favorite), potato soup, cinnamon and sugar, honey, chocolate, garlic shrimp, black pepper, herb and tomato, or blueberry.

- Churros can be found at a few places in the Florida Disney parks, but in California, they're ubiquitous. People here adore them. **Willie's Churros** is found opposite the ice cream carts to the left of the hub as you ride the trolley to the end of Buena Vista Street. Churros are some 16 inches of warm, thin, donut-like goodness coated with cinnamon and sugar. Original churros were about 6 inches long, but Disney wanted something grander—and oh boy, did they get it! Bringing them to Disney was the brainchild of Jim Logan, who worked in the Disneyland food service for fifty years and had noted their popularity at the Long Beach Grand Prix. There are specialty flavors and limited editions sold seasonally or to commemorate special events. Dips used to be sold along with the churros but have lately been discontinued, due to messy drips!

Carthay Circle Restaurant

ADP: Yes, Cost: $$-$$$
TYPE: American, Fine/Signature Dining, Unique/Themed Dining; Lunch, Dinner

On the second floor of the old Carthay Circle Theatre is the restaurant, a tribute to Hollywood's golden age of movies. Will you need a reservation? Yes, you will. This is definitely an upscale place to dine, one of the few in Disney California Adventure. The executive chef is Andrew Sutton, the same one who is in charge of cuisine at the spectacular Napa Rose in the Grand Californian Hotel. Therefore, expect to be delighted, but don't expect that delight to come cheap. Sutton makes a point of using only the freshest of locally-sourced seasonal ingredients, so menu offerings change with the seasons and are frequently refreshed, but what follows is an idea of the kinds of menu items you might expect to find here.

Unlike many Disney eateries, lunch and dinner here have somewhat different menus with dinner being more extensive—and expensive. At lunch recently, starters included the (you-just-can't-stop-eating-them) Carthay signature fried biscuits stuffed with white cheddar and bacon, jalapeño, and apricot honey butter, a fairytale pumpkin broth, Cuban braised pork, shaved speck (deep red, thinly sliced, smoky cured pork, similar to prosciutto) and persimmon salad with candied hazelnuts and crispy Brie—yet another are-you-*kidding*-me unforgettable choice. Lunch entrees recently included a wonderful spicy shrimp a la plancha with crispy polenta, crema Mexicana, and poblano pesto, a Skuna Bay (located off Vancouver Island in the Nootka Sound) salmon with heirloom tomatoes, roasted corn, soy glazed bacon and yuzu (a Korean citrus) basil vinaigrette, and a lip-smackin' Korean Chili Glazed angus sirloin with cashew fried rice and red bell pepper sauce. Vegetarian options are available such as roasted pumpkin and sage gnocchi.

Desserts land firmly in the spectacular column with choices like the fairytale pumpkin spice cheesecake with coconut ganache and cranberry compote, an heirloom apple croustade paired with salted caramel ice cream, and the decadent Republica del Cacao silky chocolate mousse that may well make you moan out loud. Children with high gastronomic expectations can rest assured their taste buds will sing with items like crispy mini tacos, a grilled petit beef filet, orecchiette pasta, or the Skuna Bay salmon paired with steamed fingerlings and green beans.

In addition to all the starters mentioned for lunch, dinner recently offered a meltingly tender Wagyu beef and truffle ravioli with rapini (broccolini rabe), roasted root veggies, and a cabernet jus, a tenderloin carpaccio with deviled quail eggs and a yogurt-dill vinaigrette, a Carthay Circle Autumn salad with Brussels sprouts, heirloom pears, shaved blue cheese and a pomegranate dressing. To say the chef knows his stuff is a serious understatement. At dinner expect thoughtful preparations of items like sustainable fish of the day, duck breast, Berkshire pork chop, lamb, and various cuts of steaks. Sides lately were mashed Yukon gold potatoes, roasted heirloom carrots, and Brussels sprouts.

Carthay has enough non-alcoholic choices to suit most people's desires. Get your little Princess a Shirley Temple or your little Prince a Roy Rogers—and then explain who they were named after. For yourself, pick something fun from the lengthy list of after dinner drinks and dessert wines. Had a brandy Alexander lately? Classic cocktails like the Manhattan, martini, mojito, Pimm's punch, daiquiri and more should give you plenty to choose from. The wine list is quite nice, a few named for famous Disney stars like Fess Parker, Kurt Russel, and Fred MacMurray. Either lunch or dinner at Carthay is practically always a memorable, truly satisfying, even exciting event, so if you're in the mood to splurge and the prices don't daunt you overmuch, this is the best place at Disney California Adventure to indulge your desire for very special meals as only Disney does them. Carthay Circle Lounge features the same drinks and some additional bites, rolls, plates, and sweets, along with a trio of kids meals.

Clarabelle's Hand-Scooped Ice Cream

ADP: No, Cost: $
TYPE: American, Quick Service, Mobile Orders; Snacks

Lots of Art Deco special flourishes make a trip to Clarabelle's extra-fun. As you approach the end of Buena Vista Street, it'll be on your right shortly before you reach the corner. Ice cream carts are great, but this place kicks it up a notch with scoops of all your favorite kinds including a no-sugar butter pecan flavor. Get some, single or double scoops, in a fancy dipped waffle cone or in a cup. A cool thing to do is choose your flavor of ice cream bar (vanilla, chocolate, or berry sorbet), your choice of dip (milk or dark chocolate), and your choice of toppings like chocolate chips, pearls, sprinkles, Mickey's confetti, or blue raspberry "bursts" (think pop rocks). You can also order huge sundaes with toppings and extras like the Oswald, a mint chocolate chip, chocolate chip cookie hot fudge, strawberry, or mocha almond fudge, any of them served in a souvenir "kitchen sink" for about double the price. In addition to the traditional Coke beverages, you'll find Fanta orange and Barq's root beer.

Fiddler, Fifer, and Practical Café

ADP: Yes, Cost: $
TYPE: American, Bakery Cuisine, Quick Service; Snacks, Breakfast, Lunch, Dinner

In case you wonder about the unusual title of this restaurant, you'll have to go back to 1933 when Disney released *The Three Little Pigs* cartoon short. These were the names of the pig trio. On the walls of the coffee shop, look for old pictures and posters of The Silver Lake Sisters, Dottie, Dolly, and Ethel, who performed—with the same musical instruments later used by the three pigs—and sang in the 1920s and were said to have inspired Walt Disney's cartoon. There is open-air seating or you can opt to dine inside. Breakfast has lots of delicious baked goods and pastries like banana walnut bread, blueberry muffins, a variety of scones, croissants—both plain and chocolate, coffee cake, and the legendary BIG, much-adored signature cinnamon roll with cream cheese frosting.

You can pick breakfast sandwiches and wraps stuffed with some combination of bacon, eggs, sausage, and cheese or go for the spinach, feta, and egg white wrap. Even at breakfast, you'll be tempted by the desserts like the beautiful, creative seasonal cupcakes, chocolate chip cookies, iced lemon pound cake, and many more. Find plenty of Frappuccino blended beverages, Starbucks refreshers, and all sorts of espressos and coffees in various sizes. Get cold brewed coffees, too, as well as hot or iced teas. Coke products, milk, juice, water, and lemonade are on the enormous bill of fare any time.

There's no difference between the lunch and dinner menu, and you can still get the breakfast sandwiches and wraps. In addition, there are roast beef or turkey sandwiches and an apple and cheddar salad to which you may add turkey if desired. Children will find a Disney check meal, an Uncrustable with apple slices, carrots, and milk. All the breakfast bakery items plus yogurt parfaits, a berry bowl, grapes, and a veggie cup with ranch are available at lunch and dinner. There is so much on offer that just about any member of your party will be able to choose something that will hit the spot at this charming, amply-stocked café.

Mortimer's Market

ADP: No, Cost: $
TYPE: American, Quick Service; Snacks

Mortimer's is the first thing you'll pass on the right after boarding the trolley. Disney history buffs will remember that Mortimer was Walt's first choice when naming his soon-to-be-famous cartoon mouse. Lillian, his wife, suggested Mickey would be a more appealing and friendly moniker, and the result was magic. Mortimer did show up in some early Disney cartoons as a not especially likable but very large rodent foil to the popular Mickey. At Mortimer's, you'll be treated to a wide variety of fresh fruit such as seedless grapes, watermelon, and mango. Hummus, chips, pickles, or a veggie cup with ranch dip will help you stave off hunger pangs until you can stop for a meal. You'll find water, juices, lemonade, and Coke products here.

Hollywood Land

Hollywood was the name given to the movie capitol nestled in the rolling hills of Southern California. Incorporated in 1903, by 1912 the film industry was flourishing in the warm, sunny, and sparsely populated area near the Pacific Ocean where palm trees swayed and a riot of flamboyant flowers bloomed year 'round. The iconic white letters on a hill overlooking the little town were originally put there to advertise a specific housing development and read HOLLYWOODLAND. When Los Angeles decided to rebuild the aging sign in 1949, "land" was left off since the sign had come to represent the entire town, not just one housing development. The name of this land in Disney California Adventure is a nod to that history.

Walt Disney arrived in 1923 after his Laugh-O-Gram cartoon studio in Kansas City, Missouri, went bankrupt. Walt and brother Roy founded the Disney Brothers Studio and started their first Hollywood production, the Alice series merging animation with live action. This area of the park represents Walt's Hollywood of the 1930s. In fact, when it opened in 2001, it was called Hollywood Pictures Backlot, and many of the "behind the scenes" experiences there simulate what it's like to be inside the gates of an actual film studio.

Here, you'll encounter the thrilling Guardians of the Galaxy—Mission: BREAKOUT; it's located in the old Hollywood Tower of Terror. With computer-generated random ride experiences, it never gets old. For the little ones, check out Disney Junior Dance Party with all their favorite pals from Disney Junior T.V. shows. Frozen—Live at the Hyperion features a retelling of Anna and Elsa's story, a combination of live action and screened footage. Rounding out the top attractions is Monsters, Inc. Mike and Sully to the Rescue! where you jump into a taxi cab to follow Mike and Sully as they rush to return Boo to her bedroom, but look out for Randall and the Child Detection Agency. After all that excitement, there are several options for a snack or a meal here.

Kiosks, Wagons, and Carts

- An **Ice Cream Cart** next to Disney Junior has quick service snacks. The premium Mickey ice cream bars and Mickey ice cream sandwiches are ever-popular favorites, but you can try a frozen lemonade cup, a frozen banana, or a strawberry whole fruit bar, too. Water and Coke products are available. Many ice cream stands also have cotton candy. Nothing on the cart will exceed the snack price of $14.99, and most things are much less.

- Look for the cart near the Hyperion Theatre if you feel like soft, warm **Pretzels** in the shape of Mickey Mouse. They are huge and come plain, with cheese, or stuffed with cream-cheese or jalapeño cheese and cost in the $5-6 range. The cart has water and Coke products, as do nearly all of the kiosks, wagons, and carts.

- Between Monsters, Inc. and Frozen, you'll find some heartier fare at **Studio Catering**. The Most Dangerous Tacos in the Galaxy, Space Outpost Tacos, and Obviously Nachos are heavy on the extras from beef barbacoa (barbecue) to mojo marinated chicken to chipotle cream. The "dangerous" tacos have that fiery hot-hotter-*hottest* habañero salsa, so be forewarned! Try the Fanta Orange Freeze with Blue Cream to cool down. Slushes and fountain beverages are sold.

- The **Turkey Legs Cart** is opposite Schmoozies near the Backlot Stage. It's hard to resist the cured, smoked turkey legs that weigh in at about a pound and a half! No, they are definitely NOT Emu legs, contrary to what you may have heard. They're priced at about $12.50, but believe me, you'll be stuffed fuller than a Thanksgiving turkey after eating one! More than two million are sold annually between the Disney theme parks in Orlando and Anaheim. Try one for yourself and see why.

- A little kiosk called the **Hollywood Lounge** is tucked in the far corner of Hollywood Land and not easy to find. It's simply an outdoor walk-up counter for mostly adult beverages located in the old Mad Tea Party building. It offers a nice variety of specialty cocktails and is noted for the fun, glowing ice cubes. If you want a little something to nibble while you sip a drink, there's a Groot-shaped loaf of sourdough bread to share called (what else?) "I Am Bread". Discover drinks like rum island iced tea, nuclear lemonade, the mighty-rita (pineapple margarita), spinal fluid michelada, or the eye-opening bootlegger's black phoenix coffee chipotle stout—if you dare. The "lounge" also has Coke products, water, and a specialty lemonade slush. If you're looking for an *actual* lounge experience, try the Carthay Circle Lounge, however, over on Buena Vista Street.

Award Weiners

ADP: Yes, Cost: $
TYPE: American, Quick Service, Mobile Orders; Snacks

Take a turn to the left turn at the central fountain in front of the Carthay Theatre that will lead you to Hollywood Land. One of the first places you'll come to is this lip-smackin' little counter. It's directly across from Disney Junior. Expect to find everything from gourmet hot dogs to authentic street versions and sausages here. They have that satisfying snap as you bite into the crisp casing, indicative of a superior dog.

Offerings are seasonal, so these will vary depending on when you visit. In the winter, they're loaded with cheese. The cheesy celebration is a cheddar sausage with mac and cheese, spicy cheese puffs crumbled on top, and cheese curds all on a toasted bun with fries on the side. It's a relative bargain at about $10. Special Oktoberfest dogs are available in the fall.

Funnel cake fries are a decadent mix of cake, cream cheese sauce, whipped cream, and cream-filled chocolate cookies— oh, and don't forget the sprinkles. If you are a churro fan, they frequently have churro funnel cake fries with confetti cake, frosting, whipped topping, and Mickey sprinkles.

Most seasons, you can enjoy the BBQ crunch dog topped with crispy fried onions, the bacon street dog, a plain all-beef dog, and the uptown chili dog. These are each sided with film- strip fries, so named for their long and curly shape. Despite all these calorie-rich goodies, there is a Disney check meal for kids featuring a Danimals smoothie, a cutie (Mandarin orange), carrots, banana, whole grain fish crackers, and water or milk. The other kids meal is an all-beef mini dog.

Several beers and an extensive array of fancy non-alcoholic Hollywood "coolers" go well with the dogs. Seating is available behind the order window but goes quickly, so you might want to have one person in your party get a table while another places the order. Lines can be long at busy times of the year.

Fairfax Market

ADP: No, Cost: $
TYPE: American, Healthy Selections/Vegetarian; Snacks

Fairfax Market is adjacent to Schmoozies. Fairfax takes its inspiration from the legendary L.A. Farmer's Market that opened in 1934. If you're trying to eat a bit healthier or are saving up for a dinner extravaganza later, come here for hummus with snap peas and tomatoes, whole fruit, guacamole and chips, Mandarin oranges, mini Babybel cheese, old-fashioned pickles, fresh veggies with ranch dip, and the younger set's favorite GoGo squeeZ applesauce. Bottled drinks are available.

Schmoozies!

ADP: No, Cost: $
TYPE: American, Quick Service, Mobile Orders; Snacks

Everyone in Hollywood knows how to schmooze—it's simply a long, cozy, gossip session. Schmoozies! may be found directly across the street from the Animation Academy past Award Weiners on the same side of the street. Pull up a chair outdoors and settle in for your own gab-fest with one of the offerings that rotate seasonally like a cookies and cream shake or Mickey and Minnie stuffed donuts. Lots of different lemonades rotate on the menu and you can get one with a scoop of vanilla ice cream if you'd like. Smoothies are the stars here. Mango madness, make mine mocha, berry schmoozie, or a strawberry banana sensation are all deliciously refreshing options. Want to linger over coffee and close that deal? Go ahead because your choices are good ones: espresso, affogato (vanilla ice cream topped with espresso), latte, cappuccino, iced coffee, and more. Add a shot of almond, caramel, hazelnut, Irish cream, or vanilla to suit your personal preference.

CHAPTER NINE

Grizzly Peak, Cars Land, and Pixar Pier

Grizzly Peak

The magnificent California grizzly bear adorns the state flag. Before it was settled by Spain, some 10,000 of them roamed across the entire state. The subspecies is now extinct; the last one is thought to have been killed in 1922. When the theme park opened back in 2001, the area called Grizzly Peak was a slice of the bigger area called the Golden State. Pacific Wharf was also part of the area, and so was Condor Flats, which was later joined with Grizzly Peak.

Here you'll find the wildly spinning rafts of Grizzly River Run, a rock-climbing wall, zipline, trails, and rope bridges on the Redwood Creek Challenge Trail, and Soarin' Around the World, the newly updated panoramic views of breathtaking vistas around the world where you feel as if you're hang-gliding (formerly Soarin' Over California—if you haven't seen the new version, it's truly spectacular!). Anchoring Grizzly Peak is the impressive stone silhouette of a grizzly bear in profile atop a large mountain. The entire area will call to mind the feeling of being in a California National Park in the 1950s—with lots of exciting additions, of course, that you wouldn't find in Yosemite, Redwood, or Kings Canyon National Parks!

Kiosks, Wagons, and Cars

- A **Churros Cart** is parked near the entrance to the Redwood Creek Challenge Trail. Who feels like a warm, cinnamon and sugary, delectable churro right now?

Everybody? Well, okay! In case you haven't done so already, be sure to download the Disneyland app on your mobile device. It makes it (somewhat) easy to find exact locations of place to eat, restrooms, wait times at attractions, character locations, entertainment and more. You'll have to play with it a bit to get the hang of all the options and features. If you don't already have an account, you'll also need to create one.

- Just as you were getting thirsty, you'll come upon a handy **Drink Cart** near the entrance to Soarin'. If you really want to feel like you're on a camping trip, buy yourself a souvenir canteen that's filled at the time you buy it with Coke products, Dasani water, or sparking water. Just the thing to keep you cool on a warm afternoon.

- You'll find the **Gourmet Coffee** kiosk at the back Grizzly Peak on the water near the ice cream cart. Espresso, café mocha, cappuccino, café latte, iced specialty coffees, hot cocoa, hot tea, and a specialty mug to hold your beverage are all sold here.

- There is a handy **Ice Cream Cart** near the entrance to the Grand Californian Hotel. All the usual frozen goodies are stocked like Mikey ice cream bars and ice cream sandwiches, plus a selection of beverages, and the mood-brightening, fluffy pink or blue cotton candy.

- A **Popcorn Cart** is next to Soarin.' It's pretty hard to resist the aroma of hot, freshly-popped popcorn at the Disneyland Resort, so go ahead and treat yourself to some and maybe add a souvenir bucket. Coke products and water are also available. Look for a little figure turning the handle of a tiny popcorn machine on display in many of the full-sized popcorn carts. Those were originally little clowns called the Toasty Roasty Man on the early Creators' machines patented in 1893, and Disney continues the fond, old tradition.

Smokejumpers Grill

ADP: No, Cost: $
TYPE: American, Quick Service, Mobile Orders; Lunch, Dinner

You'll feel like one of the hearty breed of firefighters who keep the California forests safe if you stop by this rustic Quonset hut that serves up quick, tasty meals. A few items may run to the $$ range, but those are meant to share like the "Share Your Ears" $18.99 cheeseburger, really one big and two small burgers. Get a Mickey Birthday Sipper with a souvenir cup in the shape of retro Mickey. Those were available only to honor the Mouse that started it all for his 90th Birthday, 2019. The sippers were limited edition, one to a customer, and filled with a beverage. Other seasonal and holiday specials are sometimes offered.

Cheeseburgers with bacon, chili, or plain, spicy buffalo chicken sandwich, chicken tenders, or a BBQ jackfruit sandwich with bear paw slaw, crispy onions, and house-made sweet pickles are the "classics" here, and they come sided with waffle-cut fries or onion rings. For lighter fare, try the grilled chicken salad with black beans, corn, queso fresco, cornbread croutons, and avocado dressing—yum. A Disney check meal of chicken skewer with Danimals smoothie, carrots and drink or a burger, chicken tenders, or a grilled cheese are on the kids menu. Toddlers can get the mac and cheese with a GoGo squeeZ applesauce.

For dessert, what's better at a campout than S'mores? There's a seasonal cobbler shake, in addition to chocolate and vanilla shakes. Plenty of beers and wines go just fine with the meals, and there are lots of Coke products, juice, lemonade, coffee, punch, and milk always comes with the kids meals.

If there is any kind of dietary restriction or allergy in your party, Smokejumpers has a truly impressive modification of the regular menu listings that offer options safe for you. Choices that are milk, soy, gluten or wheat, peanuts or tree nuts, fish or shellfish, and egg free should be a great help to those who require menu accommodations.

Cars Land

Practically anyone with children is familiar with the lovable gang of characters from Radiator Springs located on Route 66– Lightning McQueen, Mater, Doc Hudson, Sally Luigi, Guido, Mack, Ramone, and more or your favorite vehicles inhabit this cozy little town that time forgot. Many places here are based on actual spots along the old highway, one of the original routes on the U.S. Highway System established back in 1926. Look for the peaks of the Cadillac Range that resemble the fins of those famous Caddies from '57 to '62.

This land was part of the big remodel that opened in 2012. Luigi's Joy to the Whirl (normally Rollickin' Roadsters, seasonally Honkin' Haul-O-Ween) returned as of Fall 2019, all ready for the holidays. It's a spinning, wild ride. If you've got a big Mater fan in your group, check out Mater's Junkyard Jamboree (seasonally Mater's Jingle Jamboree, Mater's Graveyard JamBOOree). You ride in a tractor that seems to square dance, whipping and spinning in figure eights, while the tunes are sung by Mater himself. The pièce de résistance in Cars Land, however, is the Radiator Springs Raiders, the in-demand thrill ride with multi-rider vehicles being more in-demand than the single-rider ones. It's the western counterpart of Epcot's Test Track. Even in the "off season" you'll experience long waits—unless you manage to get yourself a FASTPASS. Use the MaxPass feature on your mobile app to make same-day selections.

Cozy Cone Motel

ADP: No, Cost: $
TYPE: American, Quick Service; Snacks

Anyone lucky enough to travel across country in the early days probably remembers stopping a motels very much like the adorable Cozy Cone. Look for it next to Mater's Junkyard. In Radiator Springs, each of the bright orange cones sells a different snack treat. Cone 1: churro with dipping sauce (even though most churros don't offer that option these days) and beverages like Coke products, coffee, hot cocoa seasonally, water, and Ramona's "pear of dice" soda, Cone 2: soft serve ice cream and beverages like fountain beverages, water, and a "Route" beer float, Cone 3: seasonal treats that rotate, chili con queso with chips in a bread cone (veggie chili, too), and a bacon mac and cheese in a bread cone, alcoholic drinks like vodka and lemonade or vodka and pomegranate limeade, plus non-alcoholic ones like lemonade, limeade, and fountain drinks, Cone 4: seasonal treats that rotate, pretzels bites, cheddar and garlic bagel twist, and chocolate twist, drinks like apple freeze, frozen lemonade, Cone 5: flavored popcorn (butter, dill pickle, buffalo ranch, white cheddar, sriracha, pizza, garlic Parmesan, and seasonal rotations), fountain drinks, water, and Doc's wild grape tonic. It's an adorable venue with open-air, uncovered seats and tables with many quick, tasty snacks.

Fillmore's Taste-In

ADP: No, Cost: $
TYPE: American, Healthy Selections/Vegetarian Cuisine; Snacks

A stop at Fillmore's gas station is a blast from the psychedelic past. The geodesic, tie-dye dome recalls the swinging 60s. Here, you can load up on guilt-free goodies that are good *for* you. Find it across from Mater's Junkyard. The array of colorful, fresh, whole fruits is every bit as appealing as the geodesic dome overhead. You'll usually find oranges, apples, bananas, and seasonal fruit. Fillmore carries Babybel cheese 6-pack, cuties (Mandarin oranges) 3-pack, pickles, and assorted kinds of chips and dried fruit. Bottled beverages are on hand and on ice.

Flo's V8 Café

ADP: Yes, Cost: $
TYPE: American, Quick Service, Mobile Orders; Breakfast, Lunch, Dinner

Pull up at Flo's and you'll feel like you're paying a visit to American history when it was an exciting novelty to eat in your car. It's a lot like the actual Mel's Drive-in Diner in American Graffiti. You'll even note the presence of gas pumps at each of the fill-'er-up stations. Sit indoors in air-conditioned comfort or outdoors under a shady cover on tables and chairs. One nice feature of Flo's is the extensive allergy-free/friendly menu.

Breakfast has everything, from large, hearty entrees like the American (scrambled eggs, breakfast potatoes, bacon, and biscuit), chicken tamale, brioche French toast, to a seasonal fruit plate. Disney check meals for kids are the American or fruit plate with waffles on the regular kids' menu. Lunch and dinner have entrees like the rotating blue plate special, cheese-burger, club sandwich, tuna sandwich, pot pie, Cobb salad, and fried chicken with mashed potatoes, seasonal veggies. The sand-wiches come with steak fries. A turkey breast slider is the Disney check meal for kids, while the kid's menu has a burger, mac and cheese, and chicken "fenders" with fruit, carrots, and milk.

Vanilla, chocolate, and strawberry shakes fill the dessert niche. Beverages abound from non-alcoholic fountain drinks, coffee, milk, juice, tea, seasonal hot cocoa, and fruit punch to alcoholic wines, sangria, and beer. Nothing here is overly costly, and you can grab a quick meal any time with the confi-dence that practically any member of your group will find something filling and appealing, including those with special dietary requirements.

Pixar Pier

Pixar Studios has been a centerpiece of Disney's success in recent years turning out reliable hits like the powerhouse *Toy Story* franchise, *The Incredibles, Monsters, Inc., Inside Out, Brave, Up, Coco,* and others. The movies are lucrative on their own, but they further engender practically unlimited marketing opportunities, beloved characters to populate the parks, and attractions that call to mind exciting experiences from the film plots.

Pixar Pier takes its inspiration from the golden age of early twentieth century boardwalks along the shore. When it first opened back in 2001, it was called Paradise Pier. It received not only a new appellation but a complete make-over with the big 2012 transformation of the park. Toy Story Midway Mania! added a surprisingly appealing opportunity to aim your laser 4D at targets to see who can rack up the highest score—whether you're a video game fan or not, this one is a "blast" for everyone! It's like the old midway games where you shot at ducks, but this version adds all kinds space-age of fun. The big Sun Wheel, a tall Ferris wheel, became Mickey's Fun Wheel. You'll also find the Pixar Pal-A-Round (a swinging and a non-swinging version) and the huge, ever-popular Incredicoaster in this part of Disney California Adventure. For guests of all ages, Pixar Pier is definitely a winner!

Kiosks, Wagons, and Carts

- **Angry Dogs** is a little kiosk near the base of the big Mickey's Fun Wheel that takes its name from Anger, the furious character in Inside Out. If you're feeling daring, get an "Angry" dog, extra spicy with "hot" fries. If you're feeling just "Slightly Annoyed," there's a milder hot dog for you sided with plain chips. Bottled water and drinks are available to cool that fire!

- Remember Jack-Jack, the baby of the family of the Incredibles? He's got a cute little cookie kiosk called **Jack-Jack Cookie Num Nums** located conveniently near the Incredicoaster. There isn't a big variety, but there are several good choices: a *warm* chocolate chunk, an "Incredicookie" that's vanilla, gluten free and filled with blackberry jam, and a Jack-Jack shortbread cookie with orange frosting and an edible picture of Jack-Jack himself. Milk (chocolate, strawberry, vanilla almond, soy, and 2%) or water is sold here. The cookies are pricey at about $6 but huge and oh-so-satisfying.

- If you happen to have a yen for popcorn and you're near the Pixar Pal-A-Round, there's a **Popcorn Cart** nearby. Popcorn in souvenir or premium buckets is sold, along with Coke products and water. Just like it says on the cart, it's always "Hot and Fresh!"

- **Señor Buzz Churros** is right across from Toy Story Mania! Buzz, originally named Lunar Larry, was the romantic Latin suitor of Jessie in *Toy Story 3*, and you'll see his familiar neon green and purple colors on the charming churro stand. There's the usual cinnamon and sugar "Galaxy Churro" version, you'll also have the "Caliente Churro" choice that's spicy and red.

Adorable Snowman Frosted Treats

ADP: No, Cost: $
TYPE: American, Quick Service, Mobile Orders; Snack

Look for the Adorable Snowman on the way to the Incredi-coaster and near the Lamplight Lounge. He has crossed out his old name Abominable from the sign out front advertising his wares, ever since he turned over a new leaf and became a friendly guy. Get regular or large sized servings of soft-serve ice cream in lemon, chocolate, or vanilla in a cup or in a cone. The Pixar Pier frosty parfait has non-dairy lemon soft-serve with a blue raspberry swirl and a cherry on top—the Pixar Luxo ball colors. The non-dairy lemon is also available topped with white chocolate and called "snow-capped lemon." That one can be a little messy to eat. Bottled water is sold at this quick-serve snack shop.

Lamplight Lounge

ADP: Yes, Cost: $$
TYPE: American, Californian, Healthy Selections, Vegetarian Cuisine; Lunch, Dinner

You'll find this appealing, two-story restaurant at the entrance to Pixar Pier. There are pretty views of Paradise Bay on either level. The décor is intended to suggest that the Pixar film-makers left behind lots of interesting sketches, concept draw-ings, and toys here in this industrial-looking warehouse with exposed brick, wooden beams, and concrete.

In addition to indoor tables, you can sit outside where you're guaranteed good views of the waterfront. Do make reserva-tions if you hope to be seated during busy times of the year. Sometimes, you can find a same-day table fairly close to your seating preference, but to avoid disappointment, either call ahead or make an on online reservation. Some flavorful, interesting "bites" are available like crispy piggy wings (pork drumettes with chili-ginger glaze), lobster nachos, a carne asada (steak) roll, a crab and tuna roll, and tuna poke. The spices and add-ons are out of the ordinary and provide another dimension to the flavors of the main ingredients.

Only at the downstairs dining area—inside or outside—can you get the "bigger bites" like a curly spinach salad with warm wild mushrooms, a soft poached egg, and blue cheese toast. A chicken sandwich comes sided with malted fries, vinegar slaw, and pineapple butter. Always wanted to try ratatouille? Here's your chance. It includes eggplant and bell pepper ragout with zucchini noodles, burrata cheese (yum), and several more goodies. A salmon PLT (the "P" is for pancetta) on focaccia or the cheddar burger come with malted fries, and the grilled chicken salad has lots of tasty additions. Donuts are available only downstairs.

The Disney check meal for the kids is chicken tenders with veggies with hummus and fresh fruit, but there is a PB and J roll, pasta, and a burger slider on the menu for children as well. Clever non-alcoholic beverages have fun surprises like the 2319, a mocktail with frozen strawberry purée, cream of coconut, and pineapple juice, topped with Coke. Mint to be, goofball island, and infinity fizz are more good choices.

The regular cocktail menu is very long and has just about all the drinks you might imagine, many with creative names. Six tentacles has Japanese whiskey, plot twist has Absolut citron vodka, Celtic cure has Jameson Irish Whiskey, and there are nearly twenty to choose from. More than a dozen draft beefs are sold in the downstairs dining area only, along with a nice selection of wines from California, France, Italy, Germany, and Oregon. This is one of the better places to dine if you're looking for an experience a bit out of the ordinary. The food is imaginatively prepared and the venue is nicely appointed.

Poultry Palace

ADP: No, Cost: $
TYPE: American, Quick Service; Snack

Look for a bright yellow, white, and purple stand next to the water opposite Toy Story Mania. The name comes from "Small Fry," a Pixar 7 minute "Toy Story Toon" where Buzz is left behind at the Poultry Palace and must be rescued by Woody and Rex. This stand is labeled a "snack" place by Disney, but you can certainly get enough for a quick meal, too. There's a chicken drumstick box that comes with two of them plus coleslaw. Add buttered or chili-lime buttered corn on the cob or a bag of assorted chips if you're still hungry. You can also choose the super-sized turkey leg, about a pound and a half of juicy, meaty, smoked goodness that has been enjoyed by so many guests. Coke products and water available at the Poultry Palace will quench your thirst. If you're craving something sweet after a snack or meal here, head over to Jack-Jack for a warm cookie. They're plenty big enough to share!

CHAPTER TEN

Pacific Wharf and Paradise Gardens Park

Pacific Wharf

You won't find attractions in this part of Disney California Adventure, but you *will* find a great assortment of places to dine. It's reminiscent of the exciting Pier 39 wharf area on the San Francisco Bay where sea lions bask in the sun on floating docks and Cannery Row in Monterrey, a district made famous by California regionalist author John Steinbeck in his eponymous novel. The water, in this case, is landlocked and not adjacent to any ocean, however. There is a "tour" of Boudine's famous San Francisco bakery, a place that has been making sourdough bread for a century and a half. You'll try a sample of the product at the conclusion. Another point of interest is the Blue Sky cellar where you can view a 3-D model of Pixar Pier, watch a video of Walt Disney explaining how "Imagineers" behind the senes create the magic, and work the controls of a simulated roller coaster. The cellar is filled with sketches, paintings, and artifacts from the creation of Disney California Adventure's Pixar Pier.

Kiosks, Wagons, and Carts

- Keep your eyes open for a big, bright blue truck with a red awning adjacent to Cocina Cucamonga. **Karl Strauss Handcrafted Beer** has a nice assortment of beers that include Pilsner, ales, and seasonal beer. Grab a generously-sized Mickey pretzel to go with the beer, plain or stuffed with jalapeño or cheddar cheese. A cup of extra cheese for dipping is available, too.

Alfresco Tasting Terrace

ADP: Yes, Cost: $-$$
TYPE: American Cuisine, Bars and Lounges; Lounge

A secluded, outdoor patio allows you to "get away from it all" and relax with a bite to eat and a glass of wine or a creative cocktail as you overlook Radiator Springs, the little town made famous in the *Cars* franchise. The meatballs marinara come with chunky marinara sauce, mozzarella, and Parmesan. There's a sundried tomato flatbread, a chicken Caesar piadina (thin Italian flatbread), bruschetta, a sausage and arugula flatbread, plus the delightful charcuterie and cheese board that pairs so nicely with the drinks. There are plenty of non-alcoholic options. Maybe the kids would enjoy an Ariel or Lightning McQueen Punch—both come with a clip-on glowing light. Coffee, tea, Coke products, and more are on the menu. The Disney family of wines are from California and are sold by the bottle or the glass. A full two dozen jazzy cocktails will give you a lot to choose from. Some are familiar like sangria or Irish coffee, while others are wild and crazy like the apricot "glow-tini," spicy watermelon Margarita, and fun wheel.

Cocina Cucamonga Mexican Grill

ADP: Yes, Cost: $$
TYPE: Mexican, Mobile Orders; Lunch, Dinner

This Mexican kitchen is at the end of the wharf closest to Pixar Place. More likely you've heard Bugs Bunny, not Mickey Mouse, mention Cucamonga, a city in southern California, so I'm not sure why that name was chosen. Nothing is too expensive.

Try the fish tacos for a popular Latin entrée, but be wary of the habañero sauce—it is extremely H-O-T! The plate of street tacos offers a choice of steak, pork, or chicken sided with cilantro-lime rice and black beans with queso fresco. The cocina bowl (it simply means kitchen) is similar but it is only meat (or potato cakes) with no taco shells. There's a chicken salad, a pork pastor torte, or a marinated half-chicken plate, and the sides are chips and salsa, fruit salad, or guacamole with chips. Disney check meals include a taco, bowl, or cheese quesadilla with sides, plus there's a toddler meal of chicken and rice.

Seasonal Margaritas, beer, and Micheladas are joined by a long list of fresh juices, coffee, tea, milk, Coke products, and hot cocoa in season. You'll find many allergy-free versions of the Mexican specialties for those sensitive to gluten/wheat, eggs, fish/shellfish, peanut/tree nut, or soy. Not all restaurants offer so many allergy-free menu items, but this helpful trend is one you'll find at many of the Disney restaurants these days. It's a welcome change!

Ghirardelli Soda Fountain and Chocolate Shop

ADP: Yes, Cost: $$
TYPE: American Cuisine; Snack

Some of us remember the old Ghirardelli chocolate factory overlooking the San Francisco Bay back when it was a working business. In 1965, the complex of buildings was declared a national landmark and actual production moved to San Leandro. Now, of course, it's a high-end shopping area, but the ice cream and chocolate shop there is very much like this one, and the quality is top-notch. If you can't make it up to the Bay Area, stop here for an authentic taste of San Francisco.

About fifteen sundaes with names that call to mind landmarks of the City by the Bay combine delicious ice cream with as many fancy toppings and extras as you could want. There's the Golden Gate banana split, Treasure Island warm brownie sundae, ocean beach sea salt caramel sundae, strike it rich butterscotch hot fudge sundae (butter pecan and vanilla ice cream, almonds, handmade hot fudge, whipped cream, and a cherry), twin peaks marshmallow hot fudge sundae, and more! The painted ladies (that's what locals call those gloriously colorful old Victorian houses that still dot the city) come as a midnight reverie with lots of dark chocolate and the intense 72% twilight delight chocolate, midnight bliss, or espresso escape.

Almost twenty varieties of shakes and floats are served in this charming soda shop in various sizes to suit most guests. If you simply want a refreshing scoop or two of ice cream, Ghiradelli's has you covered with cake, sugar, or waffle cones. You can order fancy toppings, all of those available on the sundae menu, or side your selection with a dipped strawberry in season, a brownie, or a chocolate chip cookie.

Hot chocolate comes many ways, some made with melted Ghirardelli chocolate chips, and all sorts of coffee specialty drinks pair well with the sweet treats. Soft drinks, milk (and chocolate milk, naturally), tea, water also add to the extensive menu. The heavenly smell alone makes this special spot worth a visit!

Lucky Fortune Cookery

ADP: Yes, Cost: $
TYPE: Pacific Rim/Asian Cuisine, Quick Service, Mobile Orders; Lunch, Dinner

For a fast lunch or dinner, you can count on Lucky to take good care of you. Walk up to the counter and you'll find the entrées are an Asian rice bowl with chicken, beef, or tofu. Sometimes, especially during busy seasons, something new is added like noodles. Sides are chicken and vegetable potstickers steamed with dipping sauce, fresh mango slices, and chilled edamame. There's a Disney check kids meal, brown rice and chicken.

Sapporo lager, fountain drinks, tea, juices, coffee, and milk. The choices are few, but you have the option to personalize by choosing your protein and your sauce: Mandarin orange, spicy Korean, Thai coconut curry, and teriyaki. They have chopsticks, so sit under a covered awning beneath Japanese paper lanterns and enjoy your fresh, hot Asian meal. Lucky has all the allergy free menu options available—be sure to look for them if someone in your party has food allergies or sensitivity.

Mendocino Terrace

ADP: Yes, Cost: $
TYPE: American Cuisine, Bars and Lounges, Table Service; Lounge

As you sit on the patio close to the Blue Sky Cellar, you'll hear the sounds of a fountain nearby. Here's a chance to consult with an expert on wine to select something special. There is an Italian cold cuts plate and a cheese plate if you're feeling peckish. There are lots of varieties of bottled beers and ciders. Wine is the main event here, however. Flights of it are available for those who would like to sample several kinds. The choices here are international. There are a great many wines from California and Oregon, but you'll also find New Zealand, France,

Italy, and Germany represented. Whites, reds, rosés, sparkling wines, and port wines will offer you a tremendous selection from which to choose.

Pacific Wharf Café

ADP: Yes, Cost: $
TYPE: American, California Cuisine, Quick Service, Mobile Orders; Lunch, Dinner

What a great spot to take a load off, kick back, and relax with a nice lunch or dinner right next to the water under umbrella tables. In cooler weather, soup in a sourdough bread bowl is hard to beat!

Some soup choices are clam chowder, broccoli and cheddar, or loaded baked potato. The lighter Chinese chicken salad with diced chicken fresh greens, wontons, almonds, carrots with a soy-ginger dressing is just right. There's a turkey pesto club on sourdough and a chicken, apple, and walnut salad with a yummy honey-lemon vinaigrette.

If you don't live here, you'll feel like a Californian eating here! Sides are fruit, a round of sourdough bread, Cheetos, Lay's potato chips, Doritos, or a freshly baked loaf of sourdough (notice a trend?). Kids can choose a Disney check meal, a turkey sandwich with Danimals smoothie, a cutie, and milk. Toddlers will enjoy the mac and cheese with GoGo squeeZ applesauce.

If you're in the mood for something sweet, try a Mickey cookie or Mickey crispy—anything shaped like the famous mouse just tastes better! Several beers, Coke products, milk, coffee, tea and juice will quench your thirst. If you've never tried the famous Boudin bakery sourdough, make time before or after your meal to take the tour adjacent to this café. You'll see why it's the top choice of San Francisco—and just about everywhere else! If you're hoping for a light meal, this may not be the best choice for you—lots of bread and plenty of mayo. It is another venue with allergy-free or food-sensitivity items on the menu.

Rita's Baja Blenders

ADP: No, Cost: $

TYPE: American Cuisine, Quick Service, Mobile Orders; Snacks

Rita's, as the name suggests, stocks Margaritas—lemon-lime, strawberry, or Grand (adds a splash of Grand Mariner). Non-alcoholic versions in lemon-lime, strawberry, and other featured flavors are available, along with chips. Rita's is adjacent to Lucky Fortune Cookery and there are lots of umbrella tables outside for sipping, relaxing, and people-watching if you need a break in your busy day. Baja means "lower" and refers to Baja California across the Mexican border, a land where fish tacos and Margaritas abound.

Sonoma Terrace

ADP: Yes, Cost: $

TYPE: American Cuisine, Bars and Lounges, Table Service; Lounge

Sit in the shade outside the Golden Vine Winery and try California craft beers while you grab a snack. Baked brie and blackberry jam with toasted crostini, a big Bavarian-style pretzel, or a meatball sandwich with melted mozzarella are great options. In addition to selections from the breweries, there are wines, cocktails, hard cider, and plenty of soft drinks to wet your whistle while you take a break.

Wine Country Trattoria

ADP: Yes, Cost: $$

TYPE: Healthy Selections, Italian, Vegetarian Cuisine, Casual Dining/Unique Themed Dining; Lunch, Dinner

If your visit to California doesn't include a stop in the Napa wine area of the state, check out this trattoria that stocks plenty of the area's best to enjoy, as many as two dozen varieties. The intent is to simulate a villa in Tuscany with tile, wood beams, and frescos on the walls. Choose an outdoor table under an umbrella or dine indoors. The food is inspired by the flavors of Italy. At less busy times of the year, you can often find a table. If you come during the busiest times, you should reserve a table in advance.

Start your meal with a Caprese salad or a rustic bruschetta. If you happen to be a fan of fried calamari, get it lightly breaded with haricot verts (green beans) and pepperoncini ailoi. Apps also include a pretty *and* tasty Italian salad with olives, Roma tomatoes, cucumbers, and shaved Parmesan with a red wine vinaigrette or you might choose a soup of the day with fresh, seasonal ingredients.

There are close to a dozen entrées. Lots of great pasta dishes such a fettuccine shrimp Alfredo, lasagne rustica, spaghetti Bolognese, linguine alla Congolese, and a couple of additional varieties of spaghetti are appropriate picks at Wine Country Trattoria. Count on finding beef, chicken, salmon dishes, and there is a light Tuscan salad with shrimp. If you haven't tried authentic osso bucco and want to give it a taste, it's slow-braised lamb, not the more usual veal, with polenta and seasonal veggies. The chicken parm (fried chicken breast topped with marinara and mozzerella) is always very tasty and filling when served over spaghetti, especially if you're not counting calories.

Tiramisù is in the same category—delicious but definitely a splurge: layers of rum and coffee-soaked lady fingers, marscapone, whipped cream, and sprinkled all over with cocoa powder. It's a little taste of heaven right here in Wine Country. Seasonal panna cotta is another dessert option.

Disney check kids meals include a fresh fruit, celery, and carrot app with a grilled chicken breast, pasta prepared to order, or fish of the day. The kids menu has cheese or pepperoni pizza.

To accompany all the delicious Italian food there are two wine flights, one with wines from California and the other with Italian wines. A fruity red sangria is on the wine menu, too. You can order more than two dozen kinds of wine by the glass. Wine Country Trattoria is a relaxing dining experience and the food is pleasant and plentiful. If you find yourself on the Wharf at mealtime, this table service establishment is a good choice for a full course meal.

Paradise Gardens Park

In 2001 when DCA first opened, Pixar Pier was called Paradise Pier, and Paradise Gardens was part of it. Today, this area calls to mind the seaside parks so beloved of Victorians who strolled the boardwalks to see and be seen while enjoying a summer sojourn at the shore. This busy area is filled with attractions including Goody's Sky school, Goofy's Glider (a wild mouse-type roller coaster), The Little Mermaid: Ariel's Undersea Adventure, Silly Symphony Swings, Golden Zephyr (silver bullet rockets), and Jumpin' Jellyfish. There's also a very cool "hydrotechnic show" called World of Color, a nod to the old Sunday night Disney television program, that combines elements of water and fireworks. Over a thousand jets of water create mind-bending shapes illuminated by a changing palette of hues. As a shimmering mist provides the backdrop, projections of Disney characters seem to come to life in time to lively music. Don't miss this if you're here after dark! All of the places to eat here are quick and casual as befits this simulated seaside locale.

Kiosks, Wagons, and Carts

- Between the Corn Dog Castle and Goofy's Sky School, you'll see the little pink, while, and blue **Churros Cart** just as you were craving something warm and sweet. The aroma alone will guide you right to where you'll find this popular California favorite.

- A **Drink Stand** may be found near Jumpin' Jellyfish. Frozen lemonade is wonderful on a warm day, and you can also get a special "souvenir sipper" filled with the chilly treat at the little yellow and white kiosk. Coffee is available and, in colder weather, hot chocolate. They are both available in souvenir travel mugs, filled at the time of purchase if you're interested.

- A pretty blue and white **Frozen Beverage Stand** is located between the Pixar Promenade and Silly Swings. Frozen drinks in wild cherry or blue raspberry are available in either a disposable cup or one of the "souvenir sippers," filled when your purchase them.

- **Ice Cream Carts** are positioned between the Little Mermaid and Wine Country Trattoria. When you're wanting something sweet and cool, this is your place to pause. Those iconic premium Mickey ice cream bars and ice cream sandwiches are always crowd favorites, and for good reason. Try a frozen banana, a favorite beach food in this area since the end of the Second World War, enrobed in chocolate and surprisingly tasty. Frozen fruit bars and Coke beverage choices are also sold here, not to mention another seaside standard, cotton candy.

Bayside Brews

ADP: No, Cost: $
TYPE: Quick Service, Mobile Orders; Snacks

While craft beer is the main draw here, there also are soft Mickey pretzels stuffed with jalapeño or cream cheese or plain. Six craft beers are on the menu seasonally, and flights are available in case you'd like to sample several. In addition to the beers, Michelada, Margaritas (seasonal flavors), and hard cider (seasonal) are on the menu, in addition to plenty of Coke products and water. This counter is located between Silly Symphony Swings and Jumpin' Jellyfish on the water.

Boardwalk Pizza and Pasta

ADP: Yes, Cost: $
TYPE: Italian Cuisine, Quick Service; Lunch, Dinner

Behind Silly Symphony Swings is this purveyor of pizza and pasta. For hearty appetites, there's plenty to satisfy you here.

Try the Mickey pizza whole or by the slice—it's pepperoni sprinkled with onions and peppers. You'll also have cheese, veggie, or pepperoni from which to choose if pizza's what you crave, either by the slice or whole. A *whole* pizza, mind you, costs more than a whopping $40, a price that seems pretty high even by Disney standards. Lighter fare includes a chicken Caesar salad, an Italian chef salad, or give the field greens with tomatoes, blue cheese, cucumbers, dried cranberries, carmelized pecans, and golden raisins in a basil vinaigrette a try.

Pastas are simple but filling. Spaghetti with meatballs, chicken tomato pesto, or a five-cheese ravioli are reasonably priced at about $10-12 and will please most people. Some guests might simply like to choose from among the sides: Dannon yogurt, an uncrustable, whole fruit, a side salad, or string cheese. Disney check meals for kids are a turkey meatball sandwich or spaghetti with turkey meatballs. A kids meal is cheese pizza with a Danimals smoothie, a cutie, and milk, while toddlers might enjoy the "yummy cheesy macaroni" with GoGo squeeZ applesauce and milk.

Some of the meals here may have you loosening your belt, but if you had yogurt and a side salad, make way for a scrumptious Italian tiramisù—ladyfingers soaked in rum and coffee, mascarpone, whipped cream layers topped with cocoa powder, chocolate cake, or a slice of lemon blueberry cheesecake. Bud Light, red sangria, or Karl Strauss beer are the alcoholic beverages. Coke products, juice boxes, milk, coffee, tea, hot cocoa in season, and water are additional beverage choices. Boardwalk is one of those helpful places that stocks allergy-free menu items upon request, so be sure to ask if you don't see what you need.

Corndog Castle

ADP: Yes, Cost: $
TYPE: American Cuisine, Quick Service, Mobile Orders; Snacks

Look for the 1950s-style billboard showing corndog royalty flying high above the red and yellow striped awning. Few places do a better corndog than Disney. The dogs are premium all beef dipped in corn batter and fried to golden perfection. Get a hot-link or the unbeatable original, both served with either sliced apples or chips. A vegetarian option is the cheddar cheese stick, prepared in the same way as the corn dogs. Coke products, tea, coffee, and hot cocoa in season are served, too. There's a reason these corn dogs are crowned king—they rule!!

Paradise Garden Grill

ADP: Yes, Cost: $
TYPE: Asian and Vegetarian Cuisine, Quick Service, Mobile Orders; Lunch, Dinner

Behind Silly Symphony Swings adjacent to Boardwalk Pizza and Pasta is this grill stocked with fresh food choices. The menu here swings pretty wildly. Is this place searching for an identity or just shaking it up to keep things interesting!

Recently, it was strictly Asian cuisine. Now, it's switched to Mexican foods such as pork tamales, tortillas de papa (potato cakes with spinach), sirloin taco platter, a really delightful pollo verde "wet" burrito (chicken in green salsa), and a refreshing fruit salad. Close to the time you plan to visit, it would be a good idea to check the menu if you're planning to eat here, since you never know what might appear!

Currently, desserts include pan dulce Conchita, a Mexican sweet bread filled with dulce de leche, and the Coco cake, basic vanilla cake dressed up with a churro-flavored mousse and sweet cream cheese frosting. The Disney check meal is an uncrustable with GoGo squeeZ applesauce, carrots, and milk. The kids menu features a cheese quesadilla with apple slices or a steak taco with rice and beans. All the usual non-alcoholic beverage choices are available at Garden Grill in addition to several nice California wines and a couple of Pacific coastal craft lagers.

CHAPTER ELEVEN

Dining Packages and Character Dining Recap

Fantasmic! Dining Packages at Disneyland

Should you decide to partake in one of the park's dining packages, don't expect a bargain. What you can expect is a good meal and admittance to a reserved area where you can view the nightly fireworks show without camping out to save a spot for hours beforehand. The three course meals are *prix fixe*, fixed price for a set menu. Your meal includes a starter, and entrée, and a dessert. You have two options, the Blue Bayou, a bit pricier and definitely the premier restaurant in Disneyland, or the River Belle Terrace, a pretty spot outdoors overlooking the Rivers of America. You may dine at either lunch or dinner. One big perk of this package is a reservation to the Bayou, something that's not always easy to obtain. You will receive one admission to the reserved viewing area for each package you purchase. The packages do not include park admission. You must purchase a park admission ticket separately. Make your reservations by telephoning (714) 781-3463, that's (714) 781-DINE, between 7:00 am and 7:00 pm daily Pacific Standard Time. You may book a package reservation up to sixty days beforehand, and even at these prices, they go quickly!

Blue Bayou

ADP: No, Cost: $$$$
Type: American, Unique/Themed Dining, Table Service; Lunch, Dinner

- Lunch at Blue Bayou begins at 11:30 am for this package

- Lunch cost is $62 for adults, $29 for children 3-9 (price does not include tax or tip), and no charge for children under 3
- Dinner starts at 4:00 pm for this package
- Dinner costs $75 for adults, $30 for children 3-9 (price does not include tax or tip), and no charge for children under 3

River Belle Terrace

ADP: No, Cost: $$$
TYPE: American, Casual Dining, Table Service; Lunch, Dinner

- Lunch at River Belle for this package begins at 1:00 pm
- Lunch cost is $45 for adults, $25 for children 3-9 (price does not include tax or tip), and no charge for kids under 3
- Dinner starts at 4:00 pm for this package
- Dinner costs $45 per adult and $25 for children 3-9 (price does not include tax or tip), and no charge for children under 3
- You may upgrade to the premium 8:00 seating for an added cost of $25 per adult and $15 per child. If you do, you can dine while watching Fantasmic! from your table on the outdoor patio. It's a nice time-saver at the end of the day when you may be tired out. Should you decide to purchase this option, make your reservation either at the restaurant or by telephone at (714) 781-DINE.

On-The-Go Package at Hungry Bear Restaurant

ADP: No, Cost: $$
TYPE: American, Quick Service; Dinner

If time is of the essence, reserve your On-The-Go dinner before your visit to Disneyland. You have four entrée choices: salmon, barbecue chicken, blackberry barbecue pork riblets, or mushroom and leek frittata. All come wild rice and cranberry-apricot grains and a kale and garbanzo bean salad. As you pick up your meal, you'll get a ticket that grants you admission to the reserved viewing area for that night's Fantasmic! show. You need not eat your meal at the restaurant unless you want to because it's portable, but the Hungry Bear is a lovely locale to stop and eat. You are required to have a paid Disneyland admission, not included with the package.

- Pick up meals from 3:00 pm until 8:30 pm, depending on the Fantasmic! schedule that day. If you schedule your meal pick-up from 3:00-6:45 pm, you'll gain admittance to the first showing. Schedule meal pick-up from 7:00-8:30 pm, and you'll gain admittance to the second showing of Fantasmic!

- Cost is $29.99 per adult, $19.99 per children 3-9 (price does not include tax), and no charge for children under 3

Other things you should know about the Fantasmic! Dining Packages:

- Be aware that there is a no-refund/no-exchange policy

- Admission vouchers are only valid on the day scheduled

- You should plan to arrive at your select viewing area at the specific time listed on your admission voucher (you can't get in early and latecomers will not be admitted)

- Unless you dine at the River Belle at 8:00 pm, your viewing area will be different from your dining venue

- There is NO SEATING, except in cases of guests with disabilities

- Fantasmic! may be cancelled due to weather or technical problems, and if that happens there are *still* no refunds or exchanges

- Everything, yes *everything*, is subject to change without notice

- Children must be accompanied by an adult

- You must be over 18 to book dining package reservations

- Your reservation requires a credit card guarantee, and unless you call to cancel 24 hours in advance, your card will be charged $10 per person

- A $10 per person charge applies to "no shows"

Tomorrowland Skyline Lounge Experience

ADP: No, Cost: $$
TYPE: American, Boxed Treat; Snack

This package entitles you to come and go as you like. There's a balcony lounge above the Tomorrowland Expo Center where you can watch Fantasmic! from your seat and snack on seasonal fruits, cheese, and some special sweets plus your choice of hot or cold non-alcoholic beverages. Make reservations in advance by calling (714) 781-DINE.

- The Lounge is open from 8:00-10:00 pm with check-in time starting at 7:30 pm—enter at the Expo Center ramp near Alien Pizza Planet

- Charge is $50 per guest (includes tax, no tip required) and no charge for children under 3

- No discounts of any kind apply

- Menu, fireworks, schedules, pricing, and times are subject to change without notice

- Cancel 24 hours in advance to avoid a $10 per guest charge

- It's "shared seating," which means you may be seated with other guests

- No strollers are allowed on the balcony

Frozen Dining Package at Disney California Adventure

If you'd like to have reserved seating to watch Frozen, consider a three course *prix fixe* meal at the Carthay Circle Restaurant, the most exclusive place to dine in the Disney California Adventure park. The lunch includes a soup *and* salad starter, a choice of three main dishes such a petite filet of beef, a special kids menu that includes Disney check meals, and an array of decadent dessert choices. After your meal, you'll go to the reserved seating area at the Hyperion Theatre to watch Frozen—Live at the Hyperion. That means no standing in long lines to get in. If you have members of your party who want to see Elsa and Anna in action, this is the show to attend, and lunch at Carthay Circle is a great way to combine two great experiences.

Carthay Circle Restaurant

ADP: No, Cost: $$$$

TYPE: American Cuisine, Fine/Signature Dining, Unique/Themed Dining, Table Service; Lunch

- Lunch at the Carthay Circle cost is $89 for adults, $45 for children 3-9 (price does not include tax or tip), and no charge for kids under age 3.
- Lunch at Carthay Circle begins at 12:00, while the Frozen show begins at 2:00 pm

Check the long list of things to know about Fantasmic! packages because the same rules apply to the Frozen Dining Package. The show may be cancelled without notice due to technical difficulties, there are no refunds or exchanges, if you must cancel your reservation do so 24 hours before if you don't want to be charged $10 per guest, and your admission voucher is only valid on the day and time indicated.

Plaza Inn Dining Package

ADP: No, Cost: $$$

TYPE: American, Buffet/Family Style, Table Service; Lunch

Taking advantage of this dining package entitles you to a spot in the reserved, standing room only area to watch the Main Street Electrical Parade. Note that this parade only runs through September 30, 2019, at which time things will change. Always check the official Disneyland website for current parades and parade times. The world famous Electrical Parade debuted on June 17, 1972, and ran through November 25, 1996. It has been a legendary fan favorite ever since. This latest version features Mickey, Minnie, Goofy, Alice in Wonderland, Cinderella, Pete's Dragon, Pinocchio, Snow White and the Seven Dwarfs, and dancers and performers decked out in thousands of tiny lights. The finale is a salute to America.

- Lunch cost for adults is $40, $25 for children 3-9 (price does not include tax, tip not required), and no charge for kids under 3.
- Reservations between 1:00-3:00 pm receive an admission voucher for the first performance of the Main Street Electrical Parade. Current parade times are 8:40 and

10:45 pm, but they may vary. It lasts about 20 minutes and is well worth seeing!

- The viewing area is separate from the dining venue
- You may request your meal "to go" if desired when you arrive at the restaurant
- No refunds, exchanges, or discounts of any kind apply
- Everything is subject to change or cancellation without notice
- Cancel your reservation 24 hours before to avoid paying a $10 per person credit card charge
- Children must be accompanied by an adult

World of Color Dining Package

Each dining package includes a three course meal with a starter, entrée, and dessert chosen from a *prix fixe* menu plus a non-alchoholic beverage. Later, you'll watch the World of Color water jets, colorful lights, and projected images from a select viewing area in Paradise Gardens Park that is not located at your dining venue. It's standing room only except in cases of guests with disabilities. Like all other packages, you must purchase a valid park admission ticket on the day of your event.

Wine Country Trattoria

ADP: No, Cost: $$$
TYPE: Californian, Mediterranean Cuisine, Table Service; Lunch, Dinner

- Lunch prices begin at $50 for adults, $25 for children 3-9 (price does not include tax or tip), and no charge for children under 3
- Additional charges for alcoholic/specialty beverages
- Dinner prices are the same as lunch
- No discounts apply
- Anything is subject to change or cancellation without notice
- No refunds or exchanges

Carthay Circle Restaurant

ADP: No, Cost: $$$-$$$$
TYPE: American Cuisine, Fine/Signature Dining, Unique/Themed Dining, Table Service; Lunch, Dinner

- Lunch prices begin at $56 for adults, $25 for children 3-9 (price does not include tax or tip), and no charge for children under 3

- Dinner prices begin at $74 for adults, $25 for children 3-9 (price does not include tax or tip), and no charge for children under 3

- All of the same caveats noted above for dining packages also apply to this package.

World of Color Dessert Party

This "dessert" is virtually a meal in itself! A bountiful presentation of both sweet and savory dessert items is served up next to the waterfront in Pacific Gardens Park. Sparkling beverages are included in the price. This is one of the few options (the other being the dining package at the River Bell for Fantasmic!) that allows you to sit back and relax in comfort as you watch the show. You need to reserve your seat in advance at (714) 781-DINE, but you'll have an excellent view of the fireworks and water show from your table. This is a relaxing, memorable way to end your day at Disney California Adventure.

- Price is $84 and includes tax and gratuity (no separate prices listed for children)

- Each person in your party must purchase the package to receive a seat voucher

- Arrive an hour prior to the start of the show

- A separate admission to the park is required—it's not included in the price of the Dessert Party

- Cancellation of the show is possible due to weather or technical difficulties without notice, but in this case, if the show is cancelled by park management, your ticket price will be refunded.

- You are required to pay in full with a credit card at the time of booking, and in the event you can't make it, you will *still* be charged full price.

- It's "shared seating," which means you will be seated, but you may be seated with other guests.

Character Dining in the Parks

Please refer to each of the following restaurants that are listed in previous chapters for details and descriptions of what you can expect at a Disney character meal. For *any* meal with Disney characters, reservations should be made well in advance of your visit. Such events are extremely popular and always well-attended. Make reservations up to 60 days in advance by telephoning (714) 781-DINE or book them online. Guests at the Disneyland Resort Hotels have priority when booking dining reservations. Every table has time allotted to chat with each character, pose with them for pictures, and have them sign autograph books, a real plus because you won't need to track them down in the busy parks later. Keep in mind that certain characters reliably appear at certain restaurants, but appearances by any particular character cannot be absolutely guaranteed. Even so, it's a pretty safe bet to say you'll meet Minnie Mouse at the Plaza Inn, several of the Disney Princesses at Napa Rose, Donald Duck at the PCH Grill, and Goofy at Goofy's Kitchen.

Disneyland

- Minnie and Friends—Breakfast in the Park at Plaza Inn

Resort Hotels

- Disney Princess Breakfast Adventures at Napa Rose, Disney's Grand Californian Hotel & Spa
- Donald Duck's Seaside Breakfast at Disney's PCH Grill, Disney's Paradise Pier Hotel
- Breakfast and Dinner at Goofy's Kitchen, Disneyland Hotel
- Mickey's Tales of Adventure Breakfast Buffet at Story-teller's Café, Disney's Grand Californian Hotel & Spa

Acknowledgments

Thanks to my family for their love and support. Ron remains in our hearts, and is greatly missed by us all. A professorship in pediatric ocular genetics has been endowed in his name at the University of Iowa Hospitals and Clinics where he was a professor of medicine and eye surgeon for 22 years. While I was a Tour Guide at Disneyland, we spent many happy Friday "Date Nites" there. Daughter, Elizabeth, worked at Disneyland in one of the first classes of women to pilot the submarines and later at Walt Disney World on the Skyway. Liz and her brilliant husband, Amos, a former cast member on Small World, met in the College Program at Disneyland. Their daughter, Katherine, is now twelve, and son, Drew, is nine. Rob and his lovely wife Catherine are fond parents to William, now three, and Lucy, one. We've shared a great many memorable times at Disneyland, Walt Disney World, and on the Disney Magic cruise. Maybe one day, if they are lucky, the children will become third generation cast members.

Big hugs and much appreciation are sent to very dear friends Anne, Cathy, Della, Linda, Meg, Renee, and Suzanne who are so important in my life, and to delightful Book Club friends Becky, Dell, Jane, Margaret, Wendy (who was both Chip and Dale at Walt Disney World), and Sheral. Each one of these bright, kind, and lovely ladies provide me with a never-ending source of inspiration and delight, not to mention lots of laughs!

Finally, special thanks to Bob McLain, editor of Theme Park Press. Bob is an excellent editor, a provider of good ideas, and the inexhaustible curator of all things Disney. Bob knows just about everything worth knowing about the subject, and I'm happy to say this is the tenth book he has edited for me.

Index

About the Author

Andrea McGann Keech was born in Southern California and visited Disneyland often, ever since the summer it opened in 1955. She fulfilled a life-long dream by working at the park when she became a bilingual Tour Guide and VIP Hostess during college from 1969 through 1972, experiences fondly chronicled in her first book *The Cream of the Crop, Tour Guide Tales from Disneyland's Golden Years* (Theme Park Press, 2016).

After graduating, Andrea taught students in English and Spanish in grades K-12 during her teaching career. She was a member of the National Assessment of Educational Progress Committee that established Writing Standards, 2011-2018, for students in grades 3-12. She has written for a variety of national educational journals and presented at many teaching conferences.

She lives in Iowa City with Shadow and Sunny, a pair of boisterous standard poodles. After school, she plays Mary Poppins to beloved grandchildren, Katherine and Drew, and spends as much time as possible with sweet Will and baby Lucy, her newest grandchild. Other Disney titles for Theme Park Press are *The Indulgent Grandparent's Guide to Walt Disney World, Treasure of the Ten Tags—A Disneyland Adventure, 2018 Walt Disney World Dining Guide, Walt Disney World Characters 101—Your Complete Guide to Perfect Meet-and-Greets, 2018 A Mouse for All Seasons, Your Month-by-Month Guide to Walt Disney World, 50 Fun, Fabulous Foods at Disney Theme Parks: A Gourmand's Guide to the Magic,* and *2020 Walt Disney World Dining Guide.*

ABOUT THEME PARK PRESS

Theme Park Press publishes books primarily about the Disney company, its history, culture, films, animation, and theme parks, as well as theme parks in general.

Our authors include noted historians, animators, Imagineers, and experts in the theme park industry.

We also publish many books by first-time authors, with topics ranging from fiction to theme park guides.

And we're always looking for new talent. If you'd like to write for us, or if you're interested in the many other titles in our catalog, please visit:

www.ThemeParkPress.com

• •

Theme Park Press Newsletter

Subscribe to our free email newsletter and enjoy:

- ◆ Free book downloads and giveaways
- ◆ Access to excerpts from our many books
- ◆ Announcements of forthcoming releases
- ◆ Exclusive additional content and chapters
- ◆ And more good stuff available nowhere else

To subscribe, visit www.ThemeParkPress.com, or send email to newsletter@themeparkpress.com.

Read more about these books
and our many other titles at:

www.ThemeParkPress.com

Made in the
USA
Monee, IL